Roger Taylor, Freddie Mercury, Brian May, and John Deacon in 1975.

CONTENTS

At Wembley Stadium on Queen's Magic Tour in 1986.

NEAL PRESTON

Queen

EDITORIAL DIRECTOR Kostya Kennedy
DIRECTOR OF PHOTOGRAPHY Christina Lieberman
CREATIVE DIRECTOR Gary Stewart
WRITER J.I. Baker
DESIGNER Sung Choi
COPY CHIEF Parlan McGaw
COPY EDITOR Joel Van Liew
PICTURE EDITOR Rachel Hatch
WRITER-REPORTER Ryan Hatch
PHOTO ASSISTANT Steph Durante
PRODUCTION Richard Shaffer

TIME INC. BOOKS, A DIVISION OF MEREDITH CORPORATION
SENIOR VICE PRESIDENT, FINANCE Anthony Palumbo
VICE PRESIDENT, MARKETING Jeremy Biloon
DIRECTOR, BRAND MARKETING Jean Kennedy
SALES DIRECTOR Christi Crowley
ASSOCIATE DIRECTOR, BRAND MARKETING Bryan Christian
ASSOCIATE DIRECTOR, FINANCE Jill Earyes
SENIOR MANAGER, FINANCE Ashley Petrasovic
SENIOR BRAND MANAGER Katherine Barnet

EDITORIAL DIRECTOR Kostya Kennedy
CREATIVE DIRECTOR Gary Stewart
DIRECTOR OF PHOTOGRAPHY Christina Lieberman
EDITORIAL OPERATIONS DIRECTOR Jamie Roth Major
MANAGER, EDITORIAL OPERATIONS Gina Scauzillo

SPECIAL THANKS Brad Beatson, Melissa Frankenberry, Kristina Jutzi, Kate Roncinske

MEREDITH NATIONAL MEDIA GROUP
PRESIDENT Jon Werther
MEREDITH MAGAZINES PRESIDENT Doug Olson
PRESIDENT, MEREDITH DIGITAL Stan Pavlovsky
PRESIDENT, CONSUMER PRODUCTS Tom Witschi
CHIEF REVENUE OFFICER Michael Brownstein
CHIEF MARKETING & DATA OFFICER Alysia Borsa
MARKETING & INTEGRATED COMMUNICATIONS Nancy Weber

SENIOR VICE PRESIDENTS
CONSUMER REVENUE Andy Wilson
DIGITAL SALES Marla Newman
RESEARCH SOLUTIONS Britta Cleveland
PRODUCT & TECHNOLOGY Justin Law
CHIEF DIGITAL OFFICER Matt Minoff

VICE PRESIDENTS
FINANCE Chris Susil
BUSINESS PLANNING & ANALYSIS Rob Silverstone
CONTENT LICENSING Larry Sommers
CORPORATE SALES Brian Kightlinger
DIRECT MEDIA Patti Follo
STRATEGIC SOURCING, NEWSSTAND, PRODUCTION Chuck Howell
CONSUMER MARKETING Steve Crowe
VICE PRESIDENT, GROUP EDITORIAL DIRECTOR Stephen Orr
DIRECTOR, EDITORIAL OPERATIONS & FINANCE Greg Kayko

MEREDITH CORPORATION
PRESIDENT & CHIEF EXECUTIVE OFFICER Tom Harty
CHIEF FINANCIAL OFFICER Joseph Ceryanec
CHIEF DEVELOPMENT OFFICER John Zieser
PRESIDENT, MEREDITH LOCAL MEDIA GROUP Patrick McCreery
SENIOR VICE PRESIDENT, HUMAN RESOURCES Dina Nathanson
EXECUTIVE CHAIRMAN Stephen M. Lacy
VICE CHAIRMAN Mell Meredith Frazier

Published by LIFE BOOKS, an imprint of Time Inc. Books • 225 Liberty Street • New York, NY 10281

Vol. 18, No. 22 • October 26, 2018

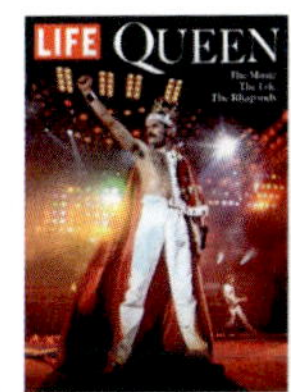

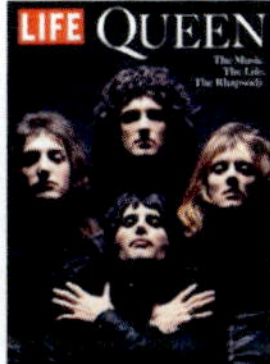

There are two covers of this Collectible Edition of LIFE.

COVERS Freddie Mercury at Wembley Stadium, London, 1986: DENIS O'REGAN/PREMIUM/GETTY
The *Queen II* album cover portrait: © MICK ROCK, LONDON, 1974, 2018

Freddie Mercury,
Hammersmith Odeon,
London, 1979.

All Hail

Through its remarkable heyday, Queen—with its singular star, Freddie Mercury, and deliciously innovative guitar player, Brian May—touched folks from across the musical and pop culture spectrum

"Playing with Queen was the biggest moment of my career. It was like living a childhood fantasy."

—**GEORGE MICHAEL,** WHO JOINED THE BAND AT THE 1992 TRIBUTE CONCERT FOR FREDDIE MERCURY

"To me, they fall into the same category as the Stones. They are totally recognizable, 100 percent successfully."

—**CLIFF RICHARD**

"Musically, they're so good. The whole group stuns you, first of all because they look so interesting."

—**LIZA MINNELLI,** ONE OF MERCURY'S TWO FAVORITE PERFORMERS, ALONG WITH JIMI HENDRIX

"Queen had a hit called 'Radio Ga Ga.' That's why I love the name."

—**LADY GAGA**

"It was hard not to get caught up in their enthusiasm. It helped of course that they were very focused and clearly very intelligent... We were all very young and reveling in the fun of the glam culture that was driving London youth at the time."

—PHOTOGRAPHER **MICK ROCK**

"Freddie took it further than the rest... he took it over the edge. And of course, I always admired a man who wears tights."

—**DAVID BOWIE**

© MICK ROCK, LONDON, 1974, 2018

"Freddie Mercury was and remains my biggest influence."

—**KATY PERRY**

"The most important figures in rock 'n' roll. Freddie's a real one-off, and that time, nobody looked like him, nobody sang like him, with the harmonies and everything."

—**ELTON JOHN**

"Every band should study Queen at Live Aid. If you really feel like that barrier is gone, you become Freddie Mercury."

—**DAVE GROHL** OF FOO FIGHTERS, ON THE 1985 DUAL-VENUE CONCERT AT WHICH 70 ACTS PERFORMED AND QUEEN'S BRAVURA, 19-MINUTE SET STOLE THE SHOW

"Pretty outrageous, true love for music. They weren't just a rock band; they incorporated lots of different music."

—**SEAL**

"The biggest band ever."

—**JOE ELLIOTT** OF DEF LEPPARD

"They've always approached music very intelligently, probably because they have so many degrees."

—**GARY MOORE** OF THIN LIZZY, REFERRING TO THE FACT THAT ALL FOUR QUEEN MEMBERS GRADUATED FROM UNIVERSITY

"[Brian May] is the governor, he's the best pop-oriented guitar player there is, really."

—**JEFF BECK**

"The name fits the band, and it fits Freddie too, it seems, because the whole thing was so majestic."

—**PAUL YOUNG**

"For a long time, I think almost all the music I played was Queen. I had a big addiction."

—**SIR JACKIE STEWART,** THREE-TIME FORMULA ONE WORLD CHAMPION

"If I didn't have Freddie Mercury's lyrics to hold on to as a kid, I don't know where I would be. It taught me about all forms of music. It would open my mind. I never really had a bigger teacher in my whole life."

—**AXL ROSE** OF GUNS N' ROSES

"Freddie is like a myth, how do you live up to that?"

—**ADAM LAMBERT,** WHO HAS TOURED WITH QUEEN SINCE 2012

DENIS O'REGAN/PREMIUM/GETTY

GALLERY

CAMERA READY

With its theatrical intensity, high work ethic, and insatiable desire to entertain, Queen left a run of memorable images

MICHAEL PUTLAND/HULTON/GETTY

The Front Man Flourishes

By 1974, Queen had finally hit the UK charts with its single "Seven Seas of Rhye." Later that year, Freddie Mercury and the band dazzled onstage at the Rainbow Theatre in London, the city that became their de facto home.

Striking a Chord

Mercury, at left, had his sights on fame since age 19, when he told longtime confidante Mary Austin, "I'm not going to be a star—I'm going to be a legend." By 1980 he and Brian May commanded the stage like rock 'n' roll superheroes.

NEAL PRESTON

Men at Work

Queen's groundbreaking studio sessions were defined by attention to detail and perfectionism—leading to creative clashes. The band recorded the 1974 album *Sheer Heart Attack* in London (here).

All Aglitter

Mercury's ever-changing wardrobe—should we just say "costumes"?—often drew as much attention as the music. In New Orleans (here), he led perhaps the most decadent album release parties of the century (for *Jazz* in 1978). In 1982, he adorned himself with featherlike arrows.

NEAL PRESTON (2)

Rhythm Section

Queen wasn't just Mercury and May, of course. John Deacon (left, on bass) and Roger Taylor (on drums) provided a steady, and sometimes thundering, backbeat. Taylor's "Radio Ga Ga" (1984) was a big hit, and Deacon's "Another One Bites the Dust" (1980) remains on the short list of Queen's greatest.

DENIS O'REGAN/PREMIUM/GETTY

Living It

Mercury seemed as healthy as ever when Queen toured in 1984 (above), but there's evidence to suggest the vivacious front man had contracted HIV two years earlier. He said he wasn't worried about it, but friends wondered if secretly he thought it was already too late.

CHAPTER ONE

ROOTS OF A REIGN

Boarding school, art school, ventures in astronomy. It's a long way to the top when you want to rock 'n' roll

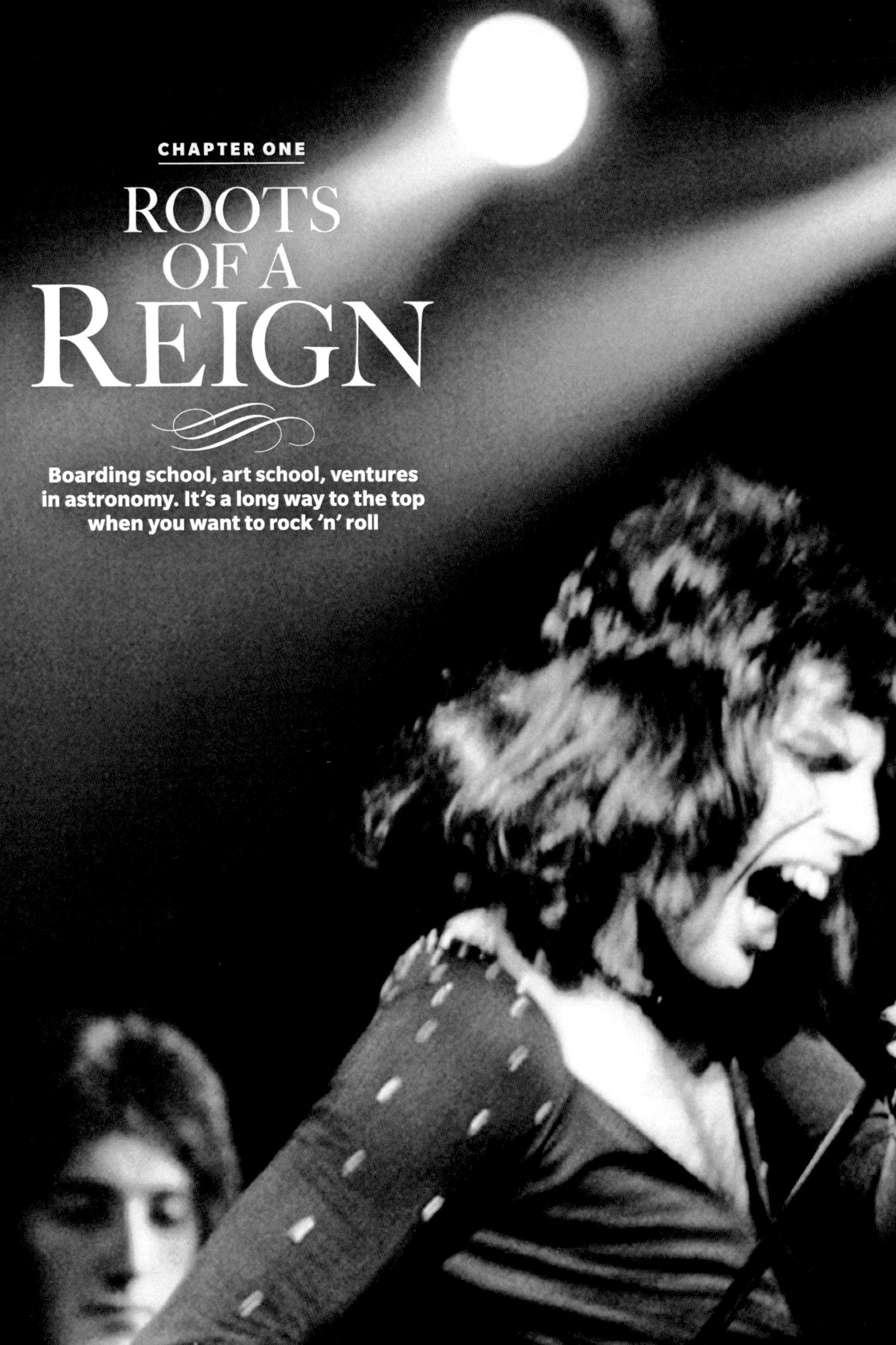

John Deacon, Freddie Mercury, and Brian May, performing at Imperial College, London, 1973.

CLARA MOLDEN/CAMERA PRESS/REDUX

In late November 1991, Freddie Mercury, Queen's legendary lead singer, lay bedridden in Garden Lodge, his Georgian mansion in London's Kensington neighborhood. Outside, paparazzi, fans, and passersby waited for a glimpse of the celebrity—or at least some confirmation of the rumors that had dogged him for years. Did he have AIDS, or didn't he?

Even on his deathbed, Mercury took pains to hide the truth. Assistants and friends learned to give him blood transfusions, eliminating the need for nurses who might have tipped the public off, and drugs were smuggled into his mansion in record-album covers. The most important of these was AZT, the best medication then prescribed for AIDS patients—and the only thing that was keeping Mercury alive. Once exploding with volcanic energy and insatiable appetites, Mercury could no longer get out of bed.

"He never really talked about being afraid of dying," said Peter Freestone, the star's longtime assistant, who was with him in his last days. "There was no point in being frightened . . . I think his only regret at the end was that there was so much more music inside him."

During Queen's fervid 20-year reign, the band released 15 studio albums, toured the world a dozen or so times, racked up numerous hit singles, and delivered what many consider the greatest rock 'n' roll performance of all time (more on that later)—thanks in large part to Mercury's musical and theatrical genius. In addition to writing a handful of indelible pop classics (the astonishingly original "Bohemian Rhapsody" tall among them), he galvanized audiences with a powerfully emotional voice while dazzling them with seemingly frivolous showmanship. Over time, Mercury appeared wearing bananas on his head ("the Carmen Miranda of rock 'n' roll," he said), an ermine gown and crown, and such comparatively mundane items as a harlequin suit, a psychedelic kimono, and a famous ballet dancer's costume. No matter what Mercury wore, he routinely whipped audiences into a fine frenzy as he strutted across the stage wielding his trademark sawed-off mike stand.

Despite his Dionysian performances (and life), Mercury was always in control—even right up to his final bow. "It was Freddie's decision to end it all," his longtime love Mary Austin

ARCHIVIO GBB/CONTRASTO/REDUX

MERCURY'S MOTHER, JER BULSARA (opposite, in 2012), raised her only son (above, circa 1958, while a student at St. Peter's School in India) in the British protectorate of Zanzibar, saying years later, "I think he always wanted to be a showman."

later said. "He knew it was coming and then he suddenly said: 'I've decided that I have to go.'"

At some point, he simply stopped taking AZT. From then on, it was only a matter of time.

THE FIRST CHILD OF BOMI AND JER Bulsara, the boy named Farrokh was born on September 5, 1946, in the British protectorate of Zanzibar, an island off the east coast of Africa. The Bulsaras were Parsis, Zoroastrian descendants of Persians who had fled to India to escape Muslim persecution. While Bomi worked as a high-court cashier for the British government, Jer looked after Farrokh, a lively child who took an early interest in music: "Folk, opera, classical, he loved them all," she later said. "I think he always wanted to be a showman."

When Farrokh was six, Jer gave birth to his sister, Kashmira, but the boy's happy home life would be short-lived. As Kashmira later said, "I only had a year of him," referring to the fact that her older brother was sent to St. Peter's, a boarding school in India, not far from Bombay (now Mumbai). "I was a precocious child," Farrokh would say many years later, when he was known as Freddie Mercury, "and

BEFORE THE WORLD KNEW Queen, Brian May (above, far right in 1967) was part of another band, called 1984, with pal Tim Staffell (far left). Two years earlier, Roger Taylor (opposite, top, second from right in the back row) played with classmates as part of Johnny Quayle & the Reactions; in '67, John Deacon (opposite, bottom, far right) played bass for the Opposition.

MARK HAYWARD (3)

my parents thought boarding school would do me good... It was an upheaval of an upbringing, which seems to have worked, I guess."

Alone in a strange country, he would cry himself to sleep at night, though he later acknowledged that the experience toughened him up. "I learnt to look after myself," he said, "and I grew up quickly."

Since his teachers found it difficult to pronounce "Farrokh," they used the British diminutive "Freddie" instead. But his classmates called him "Bucky"—thanks to the overbite caused by the four extra teeth he was born with. ("I tried to sort it out with braces but he didn't bother wearing them," his mother said. "Later he didn't want to do anything that might affect his voice.")

Freddie didn't do well academically during his roughly eight years at St. Peter's—perhaps because he was increasingly preoccupied with music. He sang in the choir and played piano for a schoolboy band called the Hectics. (Surprisingly, he was never the lead vocalist.) He may also have been distracted by his burgeoning sexuality, having discovered that he was attracted to boys—a sin akin to devil worship in Zoroastrianism. As a result, Freddie learned to hide his feelings, though some of his affectations drew notice—he had taken to calling people "my dear" and "darling," for instance.

In 1964, the violent Zanzibar Revolution forced the Bulsaras off the island, where Freddie, then in his late teens, had returned to finish his studies at St. Joseph's Convent School in 1963. Fleeing to Feltham, London, the Bulsaras stayed with relatives. Freddie was still living with his parents when he began attending London's Ealing College of Art, having decided to become an illustrator. It was an uneasy arrangement, to say the least. "He was always playing music and an elderly neighbor complained about the noise," his mother later said, "so he said it was time to go."

His destination was London, which was the place to be in the mid '60s. Carnaby Street had become synonymous with shopping and style, and the Beatles and the Rolling Stones had just conquered the world. Having fallen under the spell of the American guitar god Jimi Hendrix, Freddie no longer wanted to be an illustrator. "When I finished with the illustrating course, I was sick of it," he said. "I'd had it up to here. I thought, I don't think I can make a career of this, because my mind just wasn't on that kind of thing. So I thought I would just play around with the music side of it for a while. Everybody wants to be a star, so I just thought that if I could make a go of it, why not?"

In art college, Freddie had befriended Tim Staffell, who performed in a band called 1984 with a young guitarist named Brian May. An astronomy student at London's Imperial College, May had been playing music since the age of six. In his teens, he spent two years with his father making his own guitar, dubbed the Red Special, from an old mahogany fireplace. (May plays the Red Special—also called "the Old Lady"—to this day, using a British sixpence coin as his guitar pick.)

Unlike Freddie, May was a serious student, and he quit 1984 when he felt it was interfering with his studies. (Imperial College had given him a scholarship to study infrared astronomy.) But music was in May's blood, and it wasn't long before May decided to form another band, Smile, featuring Staffell on bass and lead vocals and Chris Smith as keyboard player. Seeking a percussionist, they tacked a sign on an Imperial College bulletin board advertising for a "Ginger Baker/Mitch Mitchell type drummer." (Baker played for Cream with Eric Clapton, and Mitchell played with Hendrix.)

The first to apply was Roger Taylor, who had played with a band called the Reaction before arriving in London to

MARK AND COLLEEN HAYWARD/REDFERNS/GETTY

MERCURY'S FIRST REAL GIG AFTER moving to London was playing with Ibex, a band he later renamed Wreckage (here, in 1969, Mercury is far left, in white). But after old pal Staffell left his and May's new band, Smile, Mercury jumped ship to take Staffell's place and, again, suggested a name change, this time to Queen.

BY THE EARLY '70S, QUEEN had a steady foursome. Said May of Mercury's early days: "I remember him dressed as the kind of rock star you hadn't seen before, flamboyant, androgynous . . . I think he was born that way."

MICHAEL OCHS ARCHIVES/GETTY

study dentistry at the London Hospital Medical School in 1967. "I remember being flabbergasted when Roger set his kit up at Imperial College," May said of Taylor's audition. "Just the sound of him tuning his drums was better than I'd heard from anyone before." Taylor got the job.

Soon the members of Smile were writing songs together and playing gigs (their auspicious debut involved opening for Pink Floyd on October 26, 1967). But for the trio, music always took a back seat to their studies. There was no future in a band, was there? Well, there might not have been—if Staffell hadn't introduced May and Taylor to his friend Freddie Bulsara in early 1969. "I remember him already dressed as the kind of rock star you hadn't seen before, flamboyant, androgynous," May said. "I think he was born that way. He was already Freddie Mercury in all but name."

Freddie was impressed by Smile—especially by the fact that they wrote their own songs, which he hadn't started doing yet—and he quickly befriended its members. (He and Taylor briefly ran a secondhand clothes stall in trendy Kensington Market.) At the same time, Freddie was playing with his own groups—notably a band named Ibex, which he had renamed Wreckage. None of these were particularly memorable outfits, and Mercury was still a musical novice, but that didn't stop him from declaring to the members of Smile: "If I was your singer, I'd show you how it was done," he said.

He got his chance soon enough. In 1970, after Smile released an unsuccessful single in America, Staffell quit to join another band—and Freddie took his place. Almost immediately, he began making changes—beginning with the band's name. "At the time it was outrageous," Freddie said of the name Queen. "It was a strong name, very universal and very immediate . . . It had a lot of visual potential and was open to all sorts of interpretations, but that was just one facet of it." (Said Roger Taylor: "I didn't like the name originally and neither did Brian, but we got used to it.")

The name also reflected the burgeoning popularity of glam rock, which grew out of British art rock in the early 1970s and was first associated with Marc Bolan and his band, T. Rex. "In those days, it was the fashion to be kind of dandyish, and I suppose we had a hand in creating the fashion," May said. "So there was this doubt in people's minds

GEORGE WILKES/HULTON/GETTY

MICHAEL PUTLAND/HULTON/GETTY (2)

ITS FIRST ALBUM, THE EPONYMOUS *Queen*, launched the group's first major tour: 31 shows mostly throughout Britain in the fall of 1973. That introduced Mercury (opposite, kneeling, and here during rehearsals) and the group to a country eager for the next big thing after the mania around the Beatles and the Rolling Stones had faded.

as to whether you might be gay or not. It was a convenient little place to be."

It was convenient for Freddie, in particular, since it allowed him to hide his homosexual inclination in plain sight. Nevertheless, the love of his life would prove to be a woman he met around this time. She was Mary Austin, a beautiful 19-year-old secretary for a trendy London fashion store called Biba. She had been May's girlfriend at first, but Freddie stepped in after they failed to click. "He was superconfident, almost to the point of arrogance," Austin later said. ("I'm not going to be a star," he would say at the time. "I'm going to be a *legend*.") Still, she was smitten—and so was he.

From the beginning, Austin was something of a surrogate mother for Mercury. She paid the rent on the dingy flat they moved into just off Kensington High Street, for instance, and supported the often mercurial musician emotionally. "She was lovely and used to come to us for meals," Freddie's mother later said. "I used to wish they had got married and had a normal life with children." Still, it was clear that Freddie would never be content with simple domesticity. When Austin suggested they have a baby together, Mercury reportedly said, "I'd rather have a cat."

"He was unique, a one-off, and anybody would have had trouble dealing with that," said Mick Rock, a photographer who shot Queen over the years—including the iconic cover of their second album, *Queen II*. "Also, he was more into his work than anything else. To compound the problem, he'd have these inexplicable crazy moments. He must have been a nightmare to work with and to live with. He knew that. He wasn't stupid. What Mary had to put up with was more than most people could take, but she never stopped loving him."

Queen performed for the first time at a Red Cross charity event in Cornwall on June 27, 1970. "We tried to hide the gaffes, but to be brutally frank, we were rough," said Mike Grose, the group's bassist at the time. He was one of several bassists the band fired—until they found John Deacon, a 19-year-old student of electronics at London's Chelsea College. As it turned out, Deacon had seen one of Queen's early gigs, but "they didn't make a lasting impression," he said. During his audition, "he hardly spoke to us at all," May recalled, but he didn't miss a beat—literally—and he was hired.

Before long, Queen's combination of rock-solid musicianship, deft song-writing, and flamboyant showman-ship—not to mention black fingernails, satin pants, ballet tights, and mascara—attracted the attention of Roy Thomas Baker, a producer at Trident Studios. He recommended them to his bosses, who agreed to let Queen record an album during off hours at Trident's Soho studio.

The process took three long years—an eternity for a notoriously impatient group. "Arguments would start about the tiniest little detail," Trident's Norman Sheffield later recalled. "They'd start screaming, shouting and chucking things. Sometimes it would blow over in a few minutes, but at other times they would stew on it, not talking to each other for a day or two. They'd always sort it out, however."

The battles were always professional.

RIDING THE SUCCESS OF *Queen II*, the band (above, in 1974, from left: Deacon, Mercury, Taylor, and May) accepted an invitation to open for Mott the Hoople's American tour, but the quartet took little joy in playing second fiddle. "They were quite arrogant," said a Hoople crew member.

MARK AND COLLEEN HAYWARD/REDFERNS/GETTY

"We were fighting to get reality into the sound," said May. "We were fighting to find a place where we had technical perfection *and* the reality of performance and sound." They also wanted everything to sound *extreme*, resulting in what Baker would call "kitchen sink overproduction."

To understand what made Queen's recording process—and therefore its sound—unique, a little history may be helpful. Before the advent of digital recording, magnetic tapes were divided into tracks, each of which could record a separate instrument or voice. In the 1950s, Frank Sinatra recorded on three-track tape. In the 1960s, thanks to technological advances, the Beatles and others recorded onto four-track tape.

The Beatles and their producer, George Martin, were the first to take full advantage of "reduction mixing" (now called "bouncing down"), which allowed them to record instruments on the first three tracks and then send those instruments, in the right sonic balance, to the fourth track. The first three tracks would then be erased to make room for more instruments or voices. "This means more opportunity for creative recording and more lush, elaborate orchestrations created by a small number of people," according to Dan Wilson, the former front man of Semisonic and Grammy-winning producer whose work includes Adele's *21*.

By the time Queen started recording, they had 24 separate tracks—"much more sonic real estate to play with," Wilson tells LIFE. "Because of that, they began to envision vastly more elaborate and dense orchestration for their records. Queen maximized the limits of 24-track recording more than any other group. Their vision was orchestral, dense, harmonically rich, bombastic—they couldn't help pushing Roy Thomas Baker off the deep end of overindulgent rock production."

Each one of May's guitar parts might be recorded four times, Wilson says, with the resulting thick blend of four nearly-identical performances bounced down to one track. Mercury's voice would be recorded multiple times in dense harmony on many tracks, then bounced down to one or two tracks. "Even after all of these efforts to create room on the tape for more ideas, the band would run out of tracks to play with, and the master tape would be bounced to another tape," Wilson says.

The more bouncing down a band does, the more tape distortion and hiss is generated. This is normally considered a bad thing, but "on loud, aggressive music, tape distortion sounds great," Wilson says. In Queen's case? "The drums exploded, and the guitars were smeared together in a resonant, harmonically rich mass, sounding more like an orchestra or a synthesizer than like guitars," Wilson says. "And the vocals crackled with urgency, like they were bursting out of the speakers."

But this "ridiculous excess" (Wilson's words) would never have worked if it hadn't been "created in service to beautiful, memorable, clever, and emotionally vulnerable songwriting, played and sung by amazingly expressive and eccentric musicians," he says. "There were probably other, even more over-the-top rock productions happening at the time, but we still listen to Queen's albums because the songs are great."

Released in July 1973, the band's first album, *Queen*, was often dismissed as a Led Zeppelin knockoff, but it contained

DAVID REDFERN/REDFERNS/GETTY

THANKS TO DAVID BOWIE'S refusing to unveil a video for his new single (he said it wasn't ready), Queen got that slot on the British show *Top of the Pops* in 1974. The show wasn't cool in the band's opinion, but their appearance on it served as a break—Queen was becoming a household name.

a startling mix of musical styles—just a taste of things to come. "We quite like to confuse people," Mercury said. "We're not really like anyone else. If anything, we have more in common with Liza Minnelli than Led Zeppelin. We're more in the showbiz tradition than the rock 'n' roll tradition." Mercury also called the band the Cecil B. DeMille of rock.

The lyrics from one of the album's songs, "My Fairy King," reportedly inspired Freddie to change his surname: "Mother Mercury Mercury / Look what they've done to me." Rewriting—and, in a sense, abandoning—his painful past, that boyhood heartache, was the ultimate act of rock-star reinvention for Mercury. "I think changing his name was part of him assuming this different skin," said May. "I think it helped him to be this person that he wanted to be. The Bulsara person was still there, but for the public he was going to be this different character, this god."

Though the album *Queen* was almost entirely ignored by critics and the public, the band Queen soldiered on, largely thanks to Mercury. He was always the most aggressive member of the band—perhaps because he had the most to lose. Though May had quit his Ph.D. thesis on interplanetary dust after the band took off, he and the three others could have fallen back on the careers they had studied for (imagine May as an astronomer, Taylor as your family dentist, and Deacon as an electronics guy). Mercury, on the other hand, was either going to be a star or nothing—and nothing was clearly not an option.

After finishing their second album, *Queen II,* the band was asked to be the opening act for the American tour of Mott the Hoople, which had recently scored a hit with David Bowie's "All the Young Dudes." Queen accepted, and though they respected the older group's experience, they refused to take a back seat to anyone. "They were quite pushy from day one," said Peter Hince, who then worked for Mott the Hoople but would go on to become a longtime member of Queen's crew. "They demanded more space onstage, they

ON THE BRINK OF IT ALL, QUEEN was extending itself beyond Europe and North America—in 1974, for the *Sheer Heart Attack* tour, the band played 26 shows throughout Japan. Here, in Tokyo, they raised a glass and a gold record for their first album. Mercury was so enthralled by the crowds in East Asia that he'd wear a kimono on stage at other shows. Later, he collected Japanese art.

DAVID TAN/SHINKO MUSIC/HULTON/GETTY

were quite arrogant. They'd got this very clear idea of what they were going to do: 'We're gonna go for it.'"

Mercury, for one, couldn't bear to play second fiddle. "Being support is one of the most traumatic experiences of my life," he later said. He was also impatient to achieve success in America—ever a key goal for British bands. "There was a bit of a do in my room," says Mott the Hoople's lead singer, Ian Hunter, "and Fred's marching up and down saying: 'When are these silly bastards going to figure it out?' Meaning the Americans. I said to him: 'It's a big country, you've got to go around three or four times before it happens. It's not like England, where you can conquer it in a day!' He was very, very impatient. It was hilarious."

In 1974, *Queen II* became the band's first album to chart in the UK—thanks to its single "Seven Seas of Rhye," which the band performed on Britain's *Top of the Pops*. The appearance may never have happened if David Bowie hadn't refused to show the scheduled video for his new single, "Rebel Rebel," claiming that it wasn't ready. It was a big break for Queen, but the band remained ambivalent: *Top of the Pops* wasn't cool.

Queen's fortunes further improved with the release of its third album, 1974's *Sheer Heart Attack*. Its first single, the Mercury-penned "Killer Queen," became Queen's first international hit—and the first track that felt uniquely Mercury's. "That was the one song which was really out of the format that I usually write in," he said. "Usually the music comes first, but the words, and the sophisticated style that I wanted to put across in the song, came first."

The innovative sounds on *Sheer Heart Attack* would be amplified on Queen's next album, 1975's breakthrough *A Night at the Opera*. "We were in a prolific stage and so much was happening with us, dear," Mercury later recalled. "We felt the need for a change of sorts and, as ever, we felt able to go to extremes." With *Opera*'s revolutionary first single, they would live up to that promise—and then some. ●

Freddie Mercury, smoldering, 1974.

CHAPTER TWO

BOHEMIAN RHAPSODY

The song that changed the game

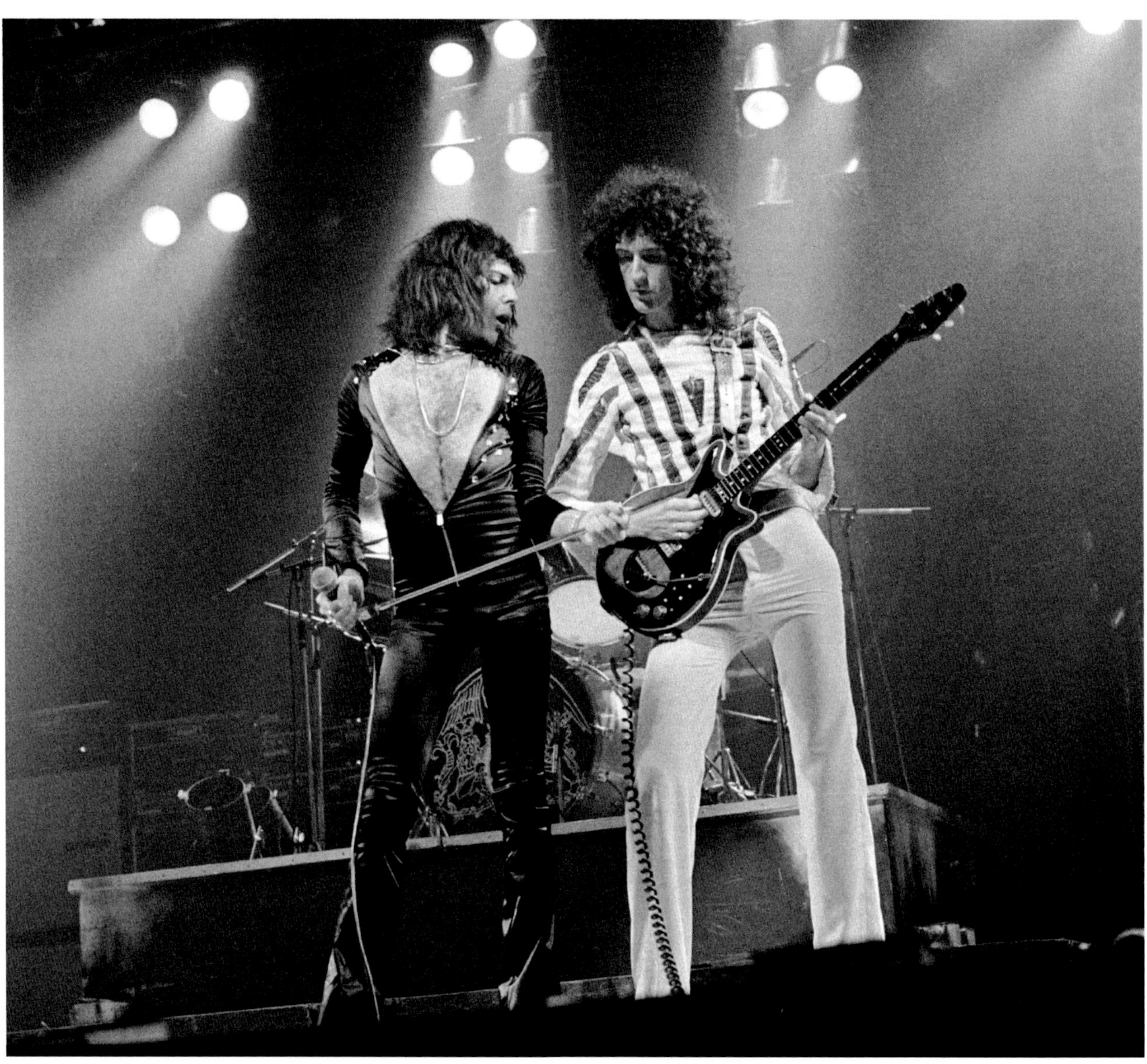

By the mid 1970s, the members of Queen were bona fide headliners—playing stadiums and touring the world—but their bank accounts hardly reflected their success. "We were not only poor, we were in debt," Brian May said. It became particularly obvious where the problem lay when Roger Taylor noticed that one of the band's managers had bought a new Rolls Royce—even as the drummer was being told not to break any drumsticks because they couldn't afford new ones. "That's ridiculous," Taylor thought. "We're selling millions of records."

Searching for new representation, Queen eventually found John Reid, who had gone from being Elton John's live-in lover to managing the singer's career. Unlike both John and Freddie Mercury, Reid was open about his sexuality: "I'm gay," he told Queen's front man over dinner one night.

"So am I," the singer said.

Mercury's internal complexities seemed reflected in the highlight of the album Queen made after Reid extricated them from their Trident contract. As usual, the band members wrote individually during a three-week rehearsal period, then shared what they'd come up with when they met at the studio. "We all brought in our ideas," May said. "From that, some would get thrown out, some would get developed, new ones would come in. And gradually there was a feeling of what kind of atmosphere on the album we were aiming for."

From the beginning, one song stood out. "Freddie said 'I've got this thing,'" said Taylor, who listened as Mercury played a tune for him on the piano, singing "Mama, just killed a man." Taylor thought the melody was "beautiful," he said. "That in itself was enough to sell it to me." But he had no idea how complicated the final composition would turn out to be. "There was so much hunger," Mercury said. "We just had so much that we want to bring out . . . and so we had all kinds of songs. And 'Bohemian Rhapsody' . . . was basically, like, three songs that I wanted to put out and I just put the three together."

Beginning in Rockfield, Wales, the recording of the song took place over three weeks in six different studios. "Freddie had a compete map of the thing

STEVE EMBERTON/CAMERA PRESS/REDUX (2)

A MONTH AFTER "BOHEMIAN Rhapsody" debuted, Queen rocked at London's Hammersmith Odeon in November 1975.

in his head," producer Roy Thomas Baker later said. "He also had notes in these books that his dad would have used for accounting at work. Freddie at the piano conducted us through it."

A full week was spent recording the song's operatic interlude. "I've just added a few more 'Galileos,' dear," Freddie would say. "We ran the tape through so many times it kept wearing out," May said. "Once we held the tape up to the light and we could see straight through it, the music had practically vanished. Every time Fred decided to add a few more Galileos, we lost something too."

The song begins quietly enough with a ballad that asks, a cappella, the question "Is this the real life? Is this just fantasy?" This is followed by the extended "Mama" ballad, then an interlude name-checking the likes of Scaramouche (a clown from commedia dell'arte), Galileo (the astronomer), Figaro (a character from the Rossini operetta *The Barber of Seville*), and Beelzebub (an ancient demon). After the hard-rock section, the song ends with the plaintive "nothing really matters to me."

"Nobody really knew how it was going to sound as a whole six-minute song until it was put together," said Baker. "I was standing at the back of the control room, and you just knew that you were listening for the first time to a big page in history. Something inside me told me that this was a red-letter day, and it really was."

The album that would feature "Bohemian Rhapsody" took four months to record and was reportedly the costliest ever made at the time. "Expensive album, enormous complexity," May said. "Even looking at it now, I wonder how we did some of that stuff." The title, *A Night at the Opera,* was inspired by the 1935 Marx Brothers film of the same name, which Baker had shown the band. "Fred and I looked at each other and said 'Good title,'" Taylor said. "We had just been doing this mock operatic thing in 'Bohemian Rhapsody.'"

"Bohemian Rhapsody" is hardly the only highlight on an album that

FIN COSTELLO/REDFERNS/GETTY

MERCURY COULD DO MORE THAN rip vocals—it wasn't uncommon to see him find a melody on the piano during a concert. Indeed, he was the whole package, and he knew it, once remarking: "The reason we're successful, darling? My overall charisma, of course."

includes such classics as "You're My Best Friend" (Deacon's song about his wife) and "Love of My Life" (Freddie's song about Mary Austin), but Queen wanted "Rhapsody," the six-minute pop suite, to be its first single. This was nothing if not controversial, since conventional wisdom held that radio would never play a song that was longer than three and half minutes. Elton John was blunt: "Are you off your head?" he said to Reid. "You'll never get that on the radio."

There was only one solution: shorten the track. "The record company, in their infinite ignorance, of course immediately suggested that we cut it down," said Taylor. The band refused. "It either goes out in its entirety or not at all," Mercury said—a risky move, given that Queen wasn't yet successful enough to throw its weight around. "It really was hit or miss," Taylor said. "It was either going to be massive or it was going to be nothing."

It was massive, of course, but it might never have happened if Mercury hadn't slipped a prerelease copy of the disc to Kenny Everett, then Britain's most popular DJ. The two men had been friends since Mercury had appeared on Everett's Capital FM breakfast show in 1974. The DJ loved the track and—ignoring strict instructions not to broadcast it—played it 14 times in two days. The result? Fans flooded the station's switchboards with calls. Some listeners arrived at the station with cash, hoping to buy the disc, which hadn't even been pressed yet.

Released on October 31, 1975, "Bohemian Rhapsody" became the band's first UK No. 1—and stayed at the top of the charts for nine weeks, inspiring the band to create a music video. "I don't know why we did it," Mercury said. "We just decided that we should sort of put it on film and let people see the film part of how 'Bohemian Rhapsody' should be." Like the song itself, the video was revolutionary—seven years before MTV went on the air.

A Night at the Opera was a critical and commercial success, topping the

MERCURY'S SEXUAL ORIENTATION was the subject of conjecture even early on, but there was no question that he loved Mary Austin (left), his live-in companion during their early twenties when the pair rented a flat in Kensington.

TERENCE SPENCER/CAMERA PRESS/REDUX (3)

UK charts and going platinum in the U.S., but this almost certainly wouldn't have happened without "Bohemian Rhapsody." According to musician and producer Dan Wilson, "the song was the peak of audacious rock overproduction, and it remains unique. It's not like after that point every pop single needed to have an operatic interlude in the middle. This was the peak, and no one climbed it again." Technical brilliance wouldn't have meant much if the song hadn't connected with listeners emotionally. "There is so much yearning and anguish and openness in these lyrics, even if they are veiled in metaphor," Wilson adds. "Just the fact that they invite so many interpretations is a sign of their brilliance."

Mercury himself always refused to explain the song, saying only that it was about relationships. "I think people should just listen to it, think about it and then decide for themselves what it means to them," he said. One theory is that it reflects Mercury's coming out as a gay man. "Sometimes the song sounds to me like a person coming to terms with his sexuality," Wilson says. "He's breaking up with a woman, suffering terrible guilt about causing her pain, but it sounds like he 'kills' his old, heterosexual persona."

It's perhaps no coincidence that Mercury finally revealed the long-standing secret of his sexuality to Austin, his partner of six years, around the time of *A Night at the Opera*. "I don't think he enjoyed hiding these things from me, and lying really to himself," she has said. "He decided ultimately that he had to tell me that he was bisexual, and I knew that really he was trying, I think, to tell me that fundamentally he'd decided that he was gay."

Having finally confessed, Freddie felt he could now live the life he'd always wanted. "The visitors to Freddie's dressing room started to change from hot chicks to hot men," May said. "It didn't matter to us; why should it?" But it would matter later, thanks to the decadence that was built into the Queen formula—on and off the stage. ●

NEAL PRESTON

CHAPTER THREE

PLAYING TO THE CROWDS

As Queen's following grew ever larger, and ever more passionate, the band embraced them right back

Brian May, sound check on show night, 1977.

ANDRE CSILLAG, COURTESY MARK HAYWARD

The houselights were killed as the stage filled with smoke and a raft of lights rose into the air. Roger Taylor mounted his drum stool and Brian May and John Deacon jumped onstage, launching into their opening chords as Freddie Mercury emerged in a shower of pyrotechnics, belting out a few songs (usually an up-tempo number, followed by a piano song and another up-tempo tune) before addressing the crowd: "Are you ready to rock?"

A thunderous "Yes!"

"Are you ready to roll?"

"YES!"

This was how Queen began its stadium performances—the band's mantra of "Blind 'em and deafen 'em" embodied by Mercury's aggressively seductive performances and his one-of-a-kind voice. Though it's often been said that he had a four-octave range, this was recently debunked by science (yes, science). He was "probably a baritone who sang as a tenor," according to a 2016 study, meaning his vocal range was in fact normal.

The study, written by a biophysicist from the Czech Republic, suggests that Mercury's secret lay in his instinctive use of both a particularly high vibrato frequency and a technique known as "subharmonics," which is also found in the unique throat-singing practiced by the Tuvan people of Central Asia. Confused? Basically, this means that Mercury could create multiple vocal tones and effects at the same time—even as he switched between a tenor's high head voice and a guttural base growl. His voice was, in other words, "a little high, little low."

This dramatic alternation between extremes was also evident in Mercury's stage show, which ranged from coy flirtation to out-and-out come-on. For instance, he often shouted, "I want to f--k all of you!" to the audience. Of course, this was all in good fun, but it was also an expression of the voracious sexual appetites that Mercury was increasingly indulging offstage. "I'm like a mad dog about town," he once said. "I'll go to bed with anything. My sex drive is enormous."

He wasn't alone. "Led Zeppelin set the benchmark for rock 'n' roll touring excess," according to one of Queen's former road managers. "But Queen took it up a number of notches. Their excess was organized like a military maneuver. The drugs were flown in to whatever city they were playing."

But the boys in the band had more than sex, drugs, and rock 'n' roll on their minds—at times, anyway. In 1974, May married Christine Mullen. The following year, Deacon married Veronica Tetzlaff (they remain together to this

CONTINUED ON PAGE 50

A DAY AT THE RACES IN 1986 SAW Mercury (front, center); Mary Austin (left); and Queen's new manager, John Reid, Elton John's ex-lover, at the Kempton Park Racecourse. Behind them are Queen's publicist, Tony Brainsby, and Taylor, and if you look closely, you can see May (third row) had sprouted a beard. Riding high in 1976 (this page), Taylor and Mercury sang together in Queen's free concert in London's Hyde Park.

KEYSTONE FEATURES/HULTON/GETTY

MERCURY WAS CONSTANTLY trying to reinvent himself, and in 1979 he turned to London's Royal Ballet to reinvigorate his and Queen's performances. Here and opposite, he attended class at the Royal Ballet. "Nobody's incorporated ballet [into rock]," he said. "It sounds so outrageous and so extreme, but I know there's going to come a time when it's commonplace." That time has never come.

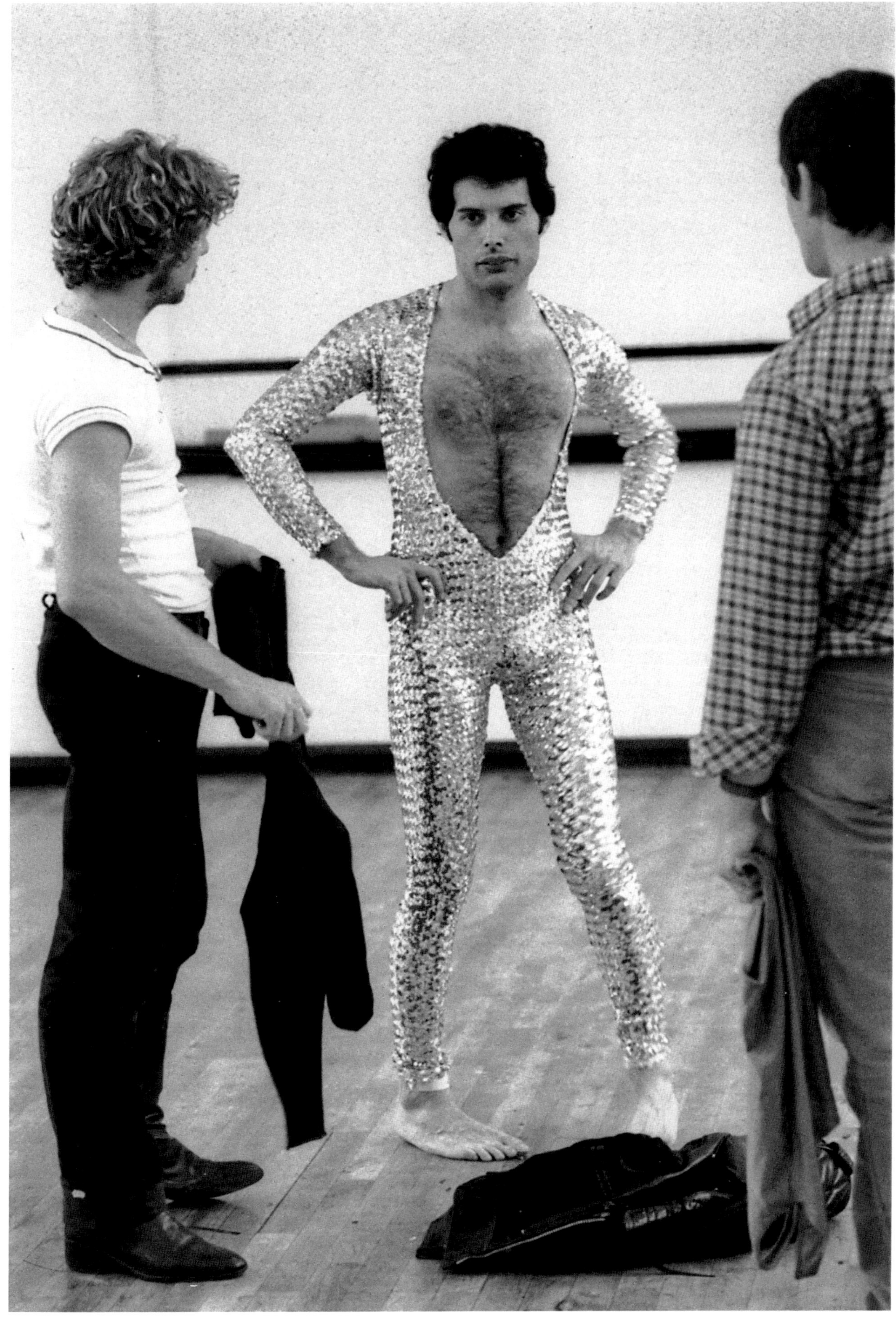

COLIN DAVEY/EVENING STANDARD/HULTON/GETTY (2)

CONTINUED FROM PAGE 46

day). In 1977, Taylor met Dominique Beyrand, with whom he eventually had two children. Always the wildest of the bunch, Mercury nevertheless remained exceptionally close to his beloved Mary Austin, whom he called his "Old Faithful." Austin continued her fierce support of the singer even after their romantic relationship ended. "She evidently filled that great hole that was left by what his parents should have been to him when he was small," said music publicist Bernard Doherty. "Instead they stuck him on a ship and sent him to school thousands of miles away. Can you imagine? In his deepest psyche he would never have resolved that."

Mercury, though, stayed close to his family. "When he wasn't away on tour, he would come home regularly," his mother later said. "He always liked my cooking, especially my dahls, sweet and sour mince, and cheese biscuits. When he was famous and had people to dinner he'd sometimes ask me to make them for him." In return, Jer enthusiastically attended her son's concerts, though she was never a fan of his style. "I didn't like his clothes and dresses, and tried to get him to cut his hair but he would explain it was something you have to do when you are in the pop world, and gradually I learned to accept it," she said. "Whatever he did or wore I always saw in him the same child I knew."

In the summer of 1976, Queen began recording its fifth studio album, the first they produced themselves. Released that December, *A Day at the Races* was an informal sequel to *A Night at the Opera* (its title came from yet another Marx Brothers movie), but *Opera* was a hard act to follow. Though Mercury's Aretha Franklin–inspired "Somebody to Love" remains a classic, the album as a whole was something of a letdown, as even Mercury admitted. "It's very difficult, especially after five albums, to come up with totally outrageous and original things," he told *NME*'s Tony Stewart in 1977.

Yet Queen remained ambitious as ever, specifically when it came to

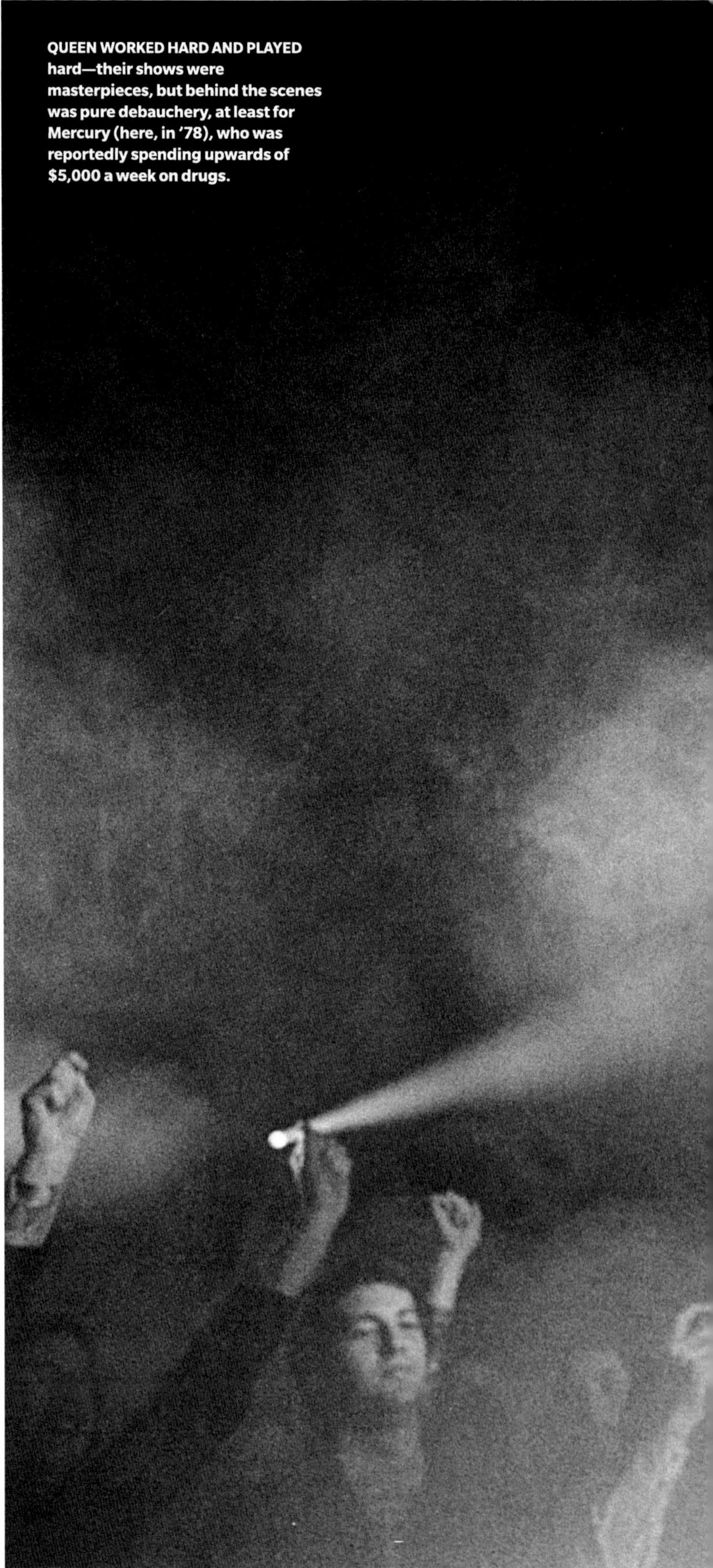

QUEEN WORKED HARD AND PLAYED hard—their shows were masterpieces, but behind the scenes was pure debauchery, at least for Mercury (here, in '78), who was reportedly spending upwards of $5,000 a week on drugs.

NEAL PRESTON

KEVIN CUMMINS/PREMIUM/GETTY

merging popular music with other art forms. "Bohemian Rhapsody" had brought an operatic twist to pop, after all—and Mercury was now obsessed with ballet, having recently performed wearing a copy of the faun costume worn by the legendary dancer Vaslav Nijinsky in the ballet *L'Après-midi d'un faune.* "Nobody's incorporated ballet [into rock]," he told Stewart. "I mean it sounds so outrageous and so extreme, but I know there's going to come a time when it's commonplace."

It wouldn't happen anytime soon. The punk and new wave movements that had taken root in New York and London—cities battling extensive poverty and a growing sense of hopelessness—were emphasizing primal authenticity in pop. "A rock gig is no longer the ceremonial idolization of a star by fans," Tony Stewart wrote. "That whole illusion, still perpetuated by Queen, is quickly being destroyed."

Even so, bands such as the Sex Pistols, the New York Dolls, and the Clash may have been influenced by Queen. "I think on some subconscious level, when 'Bohemian Rhapsody' came out, people thought, 'Well, that's as far as that will go!'" Dan Wilson tells LIFE. "Artists began pushing to be as spare and raw and unschooled as possible; the beat made a resurgence, songs had one tempo throughout; brevity, simplicity, repetition, impatient energy became the remedy for 'Bohemian Rhapsody' and other elaborate pop records."

Many old-school bands were effectively killed off by the new movements, but Queen survived. "The whole punk thing was a tough phase for us and I thought that was going to be it," Mercury said. "But if there's a challenge, we embark on it and that's what keeps us going."

Queen's adaptability is abundantly reflected in their sixth studio album, *News of the World,* which the band began recording in London in July 1977. "We'd already decided that we had saturated ourselves in multilayered production before the Sex Pistols came along," May said, "so we deliberately made *News of the World* to go back to the basics and find some vitality again."

Oddly enough, the Sex Pistols were recording their first album, 1977's *Never Mind the Bollocks, Here's the Sex Pistols,* in the same studio as Queen. One day, the band's vocalist and bassist, Sid Vicious, met Freddie, who derisively referred to him as "Mr. Ferocious." In response, Vicious sneered: "Have you succeeded in bringing ballet to the masses?"

"Dear, we're doing our best," Mercury said, pointedly flicking the safety pins on the rocker's jacket. "Tell

NEAL PRESTON

QUEEN RULED THE LATE '70S, ***News of the World*** **(1977) having gone platinum four times in the States and twice in the UK. But not everyone was a fan.** ***Rolling Stone*** **recoiled at "We Will Rock You," writing (strangely) that Queen "may be the first truly fascist rock band."**

GAY MEN IN AMERICA'S CITIES BEGAN adopting a new look in the late '70s—tight leather jackets, PVC caps, and thick mustaches, later popularized by disco sensation the Village People—which inspired Mercury to once again remake his image. Here, in Northern California in '78, he fit right in.

STEVE JENNINGS/WIREIMAGE/GETTY

me, did you arrange these pins just so?"

When Vicious stepped forward threateningly, Mercury pushed him back. "What are you going to do about it?" the queen said, and the punk backed off.

Though the band members hadn't yet written any songs for the new album, May was toying with an idea inspired by a recent concert they'd played in Stafford, England. Between numbers, Queen had heard the audience singing "You'll Never Walk Alone," the theme song for the football club in nearby Liverpool. "We thought, 'God, it's like a football match except with everyone on the same side,'" May said.

Fans were increasingly involving themselves in Queen's own performances as well. "The audience was becoming a bigger part of the show than we were," May said. "They would sing all the songs . . . they'd be so vociferous that we'd have to stop the show and let them sing to us. So, both Freddie and I thought it would be an interesting experiment to write a song with audience participation specifically in mind."

The result? May wrote "We Will Rock You," and Mercury penned "We Are the Champions," which May initially found off-putting. "The first time I heard that 'no time for losers' line I said, 'You can't do this, Fred. You'll get killed,'" he said. "But it wasn't saying that Queen are the champions. It was saying, 'We, everybody, are the champions.' It is schmaltzy and it does slightly make you shudder, but Freddie can pull that sort of thing off where most people would just make you feel sick attempting it."

Recorded in an unprecedentedly short (for Queen) 10 weeks, *News of the World* was released in October 1977. It was an immediate hit, with the double A-side single of "We Will Rock You" and "We Are the Champions" reaching No. 2 in both the U.S. and the UK. "We sort of owned [America] around the time of *News of the World*," May said. Indeed, after the New York Yankees won the World Series that fall, they adopted "Champions" as their unofficial anthem.

MERCURY'S OSTENTATIOUS LOOKS weren't always a hit in America, but on the Continent folks couldn't get enough. In 1979, Queen played nearly 50 shows across Europe, including 12 throughout Germany, with a stop in Hamburg, opposite.

WERNER BAUM/PICTURE-ALLIANCE/DPA/AP

To this day, "We Are the Champions" and "We Will Rock You" endure as high-energy anthems at sports matches, but—as May had sensed—they proved as controversial as they were catchy. "This group has come to make it clear exactly who is superior and who is inferior," wrote Dave Marsh in *Rolling Stone* in 1979. "Its anthem, 'We Will Rock You,' is a marching order: you *will not* rock us, we *will* rock you. Indeed, Queen may be the first truly fascist rock band."

Queen may have stripped their rock-star excesses from the recording studio, but they increasingly indulged them on the road. "Every morning there'd be a story going round about [Taylor] that would make you drop your knife and fork," one Queen tour manager told *Uncut*. "Then someone would stroll in and spill the beans on what Freddie had got up to and that would make you fall off your chair."

Mercury, in particular, increasingly acted out what his longtime partner Jim Hutton later called a "disproportionate obsession with physical love in adulthood." Though the singer felt his lifestyle helped inspire him, calling it "an integral part of what I was doing," promiscuity and fame could never provide what Mercury really wanted, according to Hutton: proof that he was loved. "Because audiences love me, it's hard for them to believe that somebody like Freddie Mercury could be lonely," Mercury admitted. "In fact, my kind of loneliness is the hardest. You can be in a crowd and still be the loneliest person, because you don't really belong to anyone."

Mercury's indulgences were many: He was a chain-smoker and heavy drinker, and cocaine was becoming an issue, with the singer reportedly spending up to £4,000 (about $5,000 in contemporary U.S. dollars) a week on the drug. "We'd be up for nights, sitting there at 11 in the morning, still flying high," Elton John later said. "Queen were supposed to be catching a plane and Freddie would be like, 'Another line, dear?' His appetites were unquenchable. He could out-party me, which is saying something."

That summer, the band retreated to the south of France and Montreux, Switzerland, on Lake Geneva, to record its new album, *Jazz*—partly to avoid England's punishing tax code and partly to stay out of trouble (or try to). "It was the first time we'd done an album away from home," May said. "The idea [wasn't] that there would be no distractions. Just different kinds."

MICHAEL OCHS ARCHIVES/GETTY

TAYLOR AND DEACON WERE fascinated by a polaroid camera backstage in 1977; meanwhile, on that same U.S. tour, Taylor (opposite, top) had no ax to grind with the band's axes. Bottom: The men of Queen *en déshabillé*.

Indeed. "Every night we'd go to this club on the corner that had the most amazing stripper, so we had to stop the session at eleven o'clock, watch the stripper, and then go back to record again," said producer Roy Thomas Baker. During Taylor's 29th birthday bash, Mercury swung naked from a chandelier in a Montreux hotel.

Mercury fell in love with Lake Geneva ("If you want peace of soul, come to Montreux," he once said) and was inspired to write the song "Bicycle Race" after witnessing the 18th stage of the Tour de France in the south of France. Released as a double A-side single along with May's "Fat Bottomed Girls" in October 1978, "Bicycle Race" was an odd novelty, while the album's standout (Mercury's "Don't Stop Me Now") was an unabashed, autobiographical—and, to May, alarming—hymn to hedonism. "I thought it was a lot of fun," May said, "but, yes, I did have an undercurrent feeling of 'are we talking about danger here?' Because we were worried about Freddie at this point, and I think that feeling lingers."

The video for "Don't Stop Me Now" shows Mercury wearing a T-shirt advertising the Mineshaft, one of the most notorious gay clubs in New York City at the time—and one of the singer's favorite hangouts. Located in Manhattan's meatpacking district, it featured a fake jail cell, a truck, dungeons, and somewhat more unmentionable areas. (The address is now home to the Sugar Factory American Brasserie, featuring cocktails with chocolate pairings and artisanal donuts.) "I sleep with men, women, cats—you name it," Mercury said.

May's life couldn't have been more different. "To be truthful, I was always screwed up about sex because I got married at totally the wrong time, at the beginning of all this," he said in 2011. "I'm trying to be a good husband and a good father to my kids... So that really excluded me from being wildly promiscuous. But emotionally I became utterly out of control, needy for that one-to-one reinforcement, feelings of love and discovery."

May was, in fact, romantically obsessed with a woman he'd met on the road—one of the reasons he did not indulge at *Jazz*'s album-release party that Halloween. Held in New Orleans's Fairmont Hotel, the event, dubbed "Saturday Night in Sodom," featured snake charmers, fire-eaters, naked waiters and waitresses, and much, much more.

The band's penchant for decadence was reflected in the album's packaging, which included a foldout poster showing nude female cyclists. The image caused *Jazz* to be banned as "pornographic" in some states, triggering a U.S. backlash, but Queen would soon be back on top—thanks to a song that Mercury wrote in a Bavarian bathtub. ●

MICHAEL OCHS ARCHIVES/GETTY (3)

NEAL PRESTON

CHAPTER FOUR

THE GLORY OF EXCESS

The world's biggest band kept living as large as they played

On tour in the U.S., 1980.

MARK HAYWARD

In the late 1960s, Giorgio Moroder—the Italian producer known as "the Father of Disco"—established Musicland Studios in Munich, Germany. Conveniently located near both the airport and the city's red-light district, Musicland quickly attracted the likes of Led Zeppelin, Elton John, the Rolling Stones—and Queen. Once again seeking tax asylum, the band traveled to the Bavarian capital in June 1979 to record the soundtrack for 1980's *Flash Gordon* and the album that would be called *The Game.*

Though the band hadn't written any of the new songs yet, that changed soon enough. Arriving at his hotel, Mercury was relaxing in a bubble bath when inspiration struck. Calling an assistant to bring him his guitar, he began composing. "I can't play for nuts," he said later, "and in one way it was quite a good thing because I was restricted, knowing only a few chords . . . and because of that restriction I wrote a good song, I think."

In a matter of minutes, Mercury had written a rockabilly number—a sort of homage to Elvis Presley—which he then brought to Musicland, where Taylor, Deacon, and the band's new producer, Reinhold Mack, were already at work. "My dears, I just wrote this in the bath!" the singer exclaimed. "Quick, let's do it before Brian comes!" In half an hour, they had recorded "Crazy Little Thing Called Love."

"Brian's not going to like it," Mercury said. He was right, but EMI, Queen's record label, loved it—so much so that they decided to release it in advance of the album, which the band continued recording in Munich.

In the 1995 book *Freddie Mercury . . . More of the Real Life,* roadie Chris Taylor described the band's Bavarian routine. After they finished recording—often at three a.m.—they would head to Sugar Shack (a straight club) or Mrs. Henderson's (gay), then return to either the hotel's "HH" (the "Hetero Hangout," Roger Taylor's suite) or the "PPP" (the "Presidential Poufter Parlor," Mercury's suite). There, they'd continue drinking, doing drugs, and playing board games (Mercury's favorite was Scrabble) until maybe eight a.m. "Emotionally, we all got into trouble in Munich," May said. "'Hey, let's have

DENIS O'REGAN/PREMIUM/GETTY

THE QUEEN MACHINE WAS stoked by a profusion of wardrobe choices—witness that Tokyo dressing room from 1981 (opposite) or May and his speed skater–style tights in '82, the year Queen played 69 shows across the globe for the *Hot Space* tour.

a drink after the studio.' It was nice to start with."

In October 1979, the band bought Mountain Studios in Montreux, Switzerland, as a tax shelter. That same month, "Crazy Little Thing Called Love" was released, becoming a massive international hit and Queen's first U.S. No. 1. Not least, it pointed the band in a seemingly fruitful new direction. "Queen was so eclectic that it made perfect stylistic sense for them to experiment with spare and raw dance music like with 'Another One Bites the Dust,'" Dan Wilson tells LIFE.

Inspired by the bass line from Chic's "Good Times," the Deacon-penned song became *The Game*'s second blockbuster track and yet another U.S. No. 1—thanks, oddly enough, to Michael Jackson. After seeing Queen perform in Los Angeles, the pop superstar went backstage and urged them to release "Another One Bites the Dust" as a single. "I was like, 'I don't know about that,'" Taylor confessed later. "How wrong I was."

Suddenly, Queen wasn't just *the* band to see live in the 1980s—it was "the biggest thing in the world," May said. Not surprisingly, success proved a mixed blessing. "Everything that goes with that really messes up your mind somehow," he said. "It was very excessive. I think the excess leaked out from the music into life and became a need. Queen was a wonderful vehicle and a wonderful, magical combination, but I think it came close to destroying us all."

In the spring of 1981, the band returned to Montreux to begin recording its next album, *Hot Space*—a misstep that nevertheless began auspiciously when David Bowie, who owned a home nearby, stopped by the studio. The artists started jamming, taking turns playing one another's hits—until Bowie said, "Why don't we just write one?"

PATRICK AVENTURIER/GAMMA-RAPHO/GETTY

EVERYONE WANTED A PIECE of Mercury, and he seemed to want a piece of everyone else, too. Said the singer, "I'll go to bed with anything. My sex drive is enormous." In the late '70s and early '80s, it wasn't unusual for Queen to play in front of 100,000 people each night.

CHIRULLI/RCS/CONTRASTO/REDUX

JACK GAROFALO/PARIS MATCH/GETTY

Before long, they were collaborating on the track that would become "Under Pressure." Originally called "People on Streets," it was recorded in a single evening—"quite a feat for what is actually a fairly complicated song," Bowie later said, though the musicians were reportedly fueled by plenty of cocaine and wine. Not surprisingly, there were plenty of disagreements. "You already had four precocious boys and David, who was precocious enough for all of us," Roger Taylor said in 2008. "Because passions ran very high . . . I got so little of my own way."

Mixing the song, in particular, became so contentious that Taylor walked out. Though the drummer now admits that the track is "a significant song for us," he still wants to remix it. Why was the mix so controversial on an acknowledged classic? "Different mixes affect the balance between the instruments, how aggressive the drums are," Wilson says. "Does it even sound like Queen? Freddie's voice sounds relatively natural around 0:52, during the ad libs and 'It's okay,' but Bowie sounds like he's in a tiled bathroom—very affected." To see how different mixes affect the song, Wilson suggests, compare the original album version to the remasters of 1999 (the "Rah" mix) and 2011, in which the drums are louder and more aggressive, among other modifications.

Released on October 1981, "Under Pressure" reached No. 29 in the U.S. and became Queen's second UK No. 1, but *Hot Space* would prove the most controversial album of the band's career. Determined to continue mining the vein of dance-funk they had explored in "Another One Bites the Dust," Mercury "very much wanted the music to sound like you'd just walked into a gay club, and I didn't," Taylor said. Neither did May, who called *Hot*

IN THE BOWELS OF MADISON Square Garden in '82, the chain-smoking Mercury (right) looked on with Taylor as someone named Andy Warhol—how'd this guy get in here?—sized up the rock sensations.

NEAL PRESTON

Space "so un-me." ("Body Language," the album's debut single, was the band's first without guitars.)

When *Hot Space* was released in May 1982, fans were put off by the new sound—not to mention the change in Mercury's appearance, which was readily apparent in the "Body Language" video. Gone were the blowsy frocks, flowing locks, and ballet leotards of yore—all replaced by a look known within the gay community as the "Castro Clone."

In the mid 1970s, many gay men in San Francisco and New York City began adopting a cartoonishly masculine style—including black leather jackets, studded PVC caps, and Marlboro Man mustaches. In 1977, the look went mainstream with the unlikely success of the Village People, a disco band composed of six men, each of whom represented a different gay type. The band's "construction worker," David Hodo, was a friend of Mercury's and an inspiration for his new appearance. "Some of us hate it," Deacon said of the look. "But that's him and you can't stop it." (The public didn't like it much either, with some fans throwing disposable razors at Mercury onstage, urging him to shave off his mustache.)

Mercury had always fiercely advocated change within the band, but his recent metamorphosis was purely personal. "It made it easier for him to blend in at bars, so he didn't stand out like a sore thumb," his longtime assistant Peter Freestone said. No matter where he found himself, the singer partied nearly every night, but New York City was arguably his favorite playground—so much so that he bought an apartment there in the early 1980s.

In his 1988 book, *Freddie Mercury,* Freestone describes the singer's New York routine. He'd wake around four p.m., get rid of anyone he'd spent the night with (there were sometimes as many as six), eat breakfast, and give Freestone a shopping list that inevitably included drugs. Around eight p.m., a limo would arrive to escort the singer and his entourage to the night's chosen

CONTINUED ON PAGE 70

NEAL PRESTON

RELEASED IN OCTOBER 1977, *NEWS OF the World* was quite literally a proclamation—"We Will Rock You" and "We Are the Champions" became immediate hits, indelible anthems still heard in stadiums all over the world. In the summer of '78, Mercury lit up stages across North America.

NEAL PRESTON

MICHAEL JACKSON AND Mercury (in Los Angeles in 1980, left) wrote a few songs together in the early '80s, but MJ apparently ditched his old buddy after witnessing him snort cocaine through a $100 bill. Meanwhile, in '84, Queen (opposite) donned their Sunday best for the "It's a Hard Life" music video.

MIKE MALONEY/MIRRORPIX/GETTY

CONTINUED FROM PAGE 67

club. Lather, rinse, repeat.

Surely Mercury knew that his behavior was risky—particularly given the alarming reports of a new disease that was killing otherwise healthy young homosexual men. Originally called gay-related immune deficiency (GRID), it was known to be spread through sexual contact. Was Freddie worried? Not according to his friend Paul Gambaccini, who asked him if the epidemic had made him change his ways. Mercury's answer was an emphatic no: "I'm doing everything with everybody," he replied. Gambaccini was understandably alarmed. "I felt at that moment we're going to lose Fred," he said. "And I also thought that even though he's putting up this great front, probably in the back of his mind he thinks it's too late."

In fact, the singer may have been infected during the North American leg of the *Hot Space* tour in the summer of 1982, according to Matt Richards and Mark Langthorne, authors of 2016's *Somebody to Love*. Around this time, he endured what he called "the worst flu ever," which included shingles, headaches, an upset stomach, and a white lesion on his tongue—all of which could have been among the first signs of infection.

The aftereffects of Mercury's "flu" were evident during Queen's September 25, 1982, appearance on *Saturday Night Live,* according to Richards and Langthorne. "Freddie appeared unwell," they wrote, "looking pale and drawn. His voice came in short breaths, and his vocals were shot with Roger having to back him up." (The night before the performance, the Centers for Disease Control first used the term *AIDS* to describe the disease.)

Though no one could have known it at the time, the *SNL* gig would be Queen's last appearance in the United States—thanks in part to the *Hot Space* disaster. The singer's failing health was also becoming an issue. In the winter of 1984, when Queen traveled to Munich to finish *The Works,* which they'd begun recording in Los Angeles the previous summer, Mercury started blacking out. "He got to the point where he could hardly stand being in the studio," May recalled. "He'd want to do his bit and get out."

As always, the singer had partners

QUEEN WAS ALL SMILES (AND fake breasts) in September of '84, but only a month later the band earned the scorn of just about everybody when they broke the U.N.'s boycott of apartheid South Africa by playing a show at the Sun City resort.

NIGEL WRIGHT/MIRRORPIX/GETTY

in crime. In Munich, these included Winnie Kirchberger, a local restaurateur, and Barbara Valentin, a buxom actress who had worked with director Rainer Werner Fassbinder and was known as "the German Jayne Mansfield." Despite his preference for men, Mercury began an affair with the actress, though this didn't stop him from seeing other people—including Jim Hutton, a hairdresser who would remain the singer's closest male romantic relationship.

Released in January 1984, the first single off *The Works,* Taylor's "Radio Ga Ga," was a success—thanks in part to its lavishly produced music video (ironically, the song was partly a critique of MTV). But the video for Deacon's "I Want to Break Free" was a different story. In it, the band members appear in drag as a spoof on the long-running British soap opera *Coronation Street.* "We had done some really serious, epic videos in the past, and we just thought we'd have some fun," Taylor said. "We wanted people to know that we didn't take ourselves too seriously, that we could still laugh at ourselves. I think we proved that." In the UK, people generally got the joke, but the sight of mustachioed Mercury vacuuming in fake breasts and a magenta frock was too much for many American fans, and the Stateside backlash intensified.

To make matters worse, in October 1984 Queen broke the United Nations' cultural boycott by playing the Sun City resort in apartheid South Africa—a move that alienated many fans and outraged the press. Queen's fortunes were at an all-time low. Both Taylor and May reacted by embarking on solo projects, while Mercury continued his active social life and briefly wrote songs with Michael Jackson (reportedly, Jackson ditched the collaboration when he discovered Mercury snorting coke through a $100 bill). Had Queen's reign finally come to an end? It seemed so. The band was considering breaking up. "I don't know what Queen stand for," Mercury confessed. Then Bob Geldof called. ●

CHAPTER FIVE

QUEEN, FOREVER

With an immortal performance, and a determined evensong, Freddie Mercury ensured that he—and Queen's music—would live on

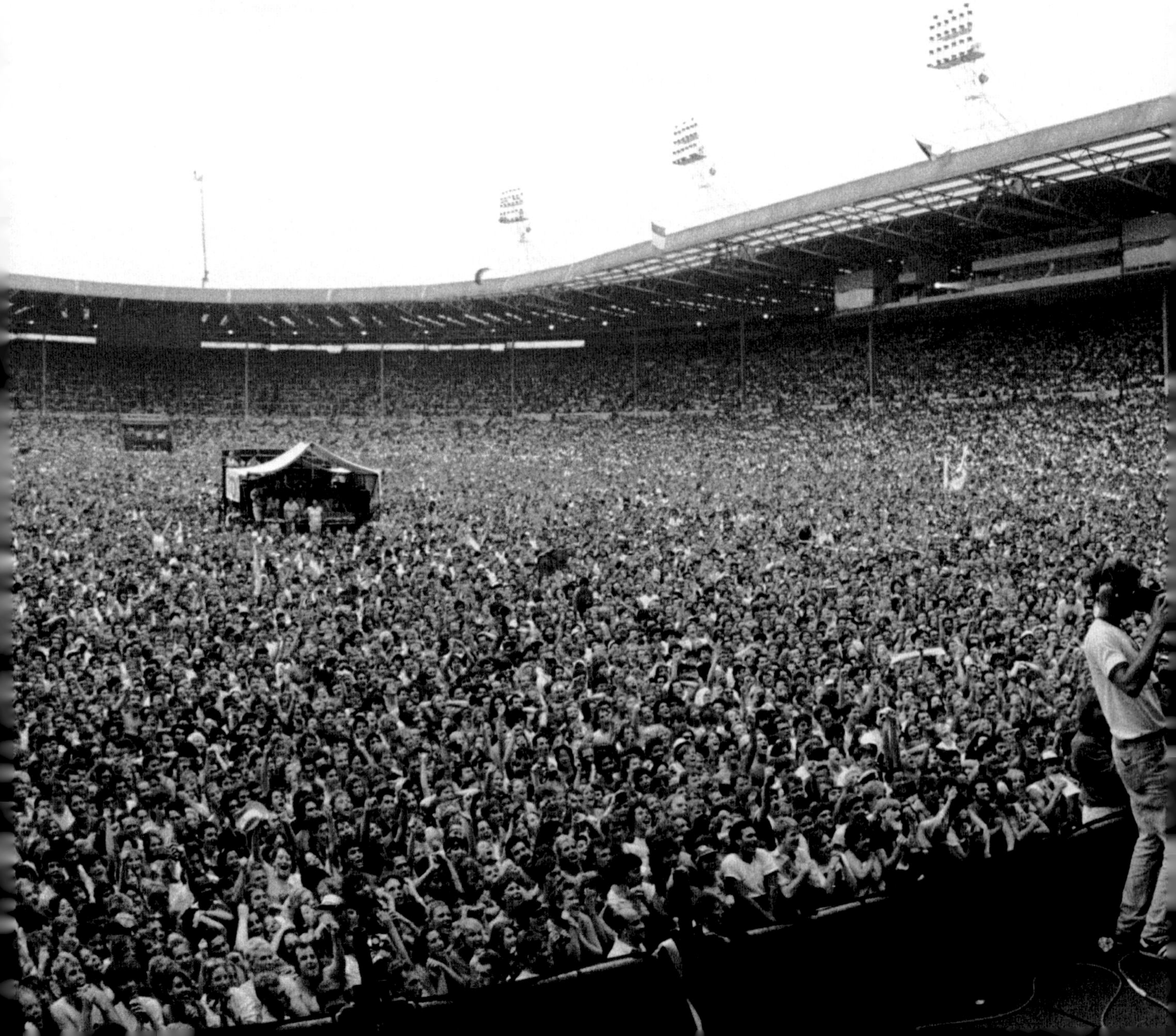

Live Aid, Wembley stadium, London, July 13, 1985.

NEAL PRESTON

MIRRORPIX/COURTESY EVERETT

In November 1984, after seeing a BBC TV report on the famine that was devastating Ethiopia, Boomtown Rats front man Bob Geldof felt trapped in a "battleground of conflicting thoughts," he wrote in his diary. What could he do to help? His band had had a brief hit with "I Don't Like Mondays" in 1979, but they had since faded from the limelight. He was not, in other words, a very big draw, but maybe other pop stars could help.

Before long, with the help of Midge Ure, the front man of Ultravox, Geldof had written a song called "Do They Know It's Christmas?" He then began enlisting a galaxy of pop stars to collaborate on the recording—including Sting, Duran Duran's Simon Le Bon, Boy George, Phil Collins, and Wham's George Michael. Collectively known as Band Aid, they recorded "Do They Know It's Christmas?" in producer Trevor Horn's Notting Hill studio, with Paul McCartney and David Bowie adding contributions remotely.

When the song was released on November 29, it went straight to No. 1 in the UK, selling a million copies in a week and eventually becoming the UK's biggest-selling single of all time. In the process, it beat the record held by "Bohemian Rhapsody"—a blow, given that Queen hadn't been invited to contribute to the single. That lack of an invitation was yet another sign of the band's growing marginalization.

Still, Geldof wanted Queen to perform at the follow-up charity event that he called Live Aid, a "global jukebox" that would take place at Wembley Stadium in the UK and John F. Kennedy stadium in Philadelphia. Queen initially dismissed Geldof's ambitious project as "pie in the sky," and their manager, Jim Beach, turned him down. "Oh, you know, Freddie's very sensitive," he told Geldof, who responded: "Tell the old faggot it's going to be the biggest thing that ever happened."

Mercury appreciated Geldof's bluntness, and Queen eventually agreed to perform—along with Bowie, Elton John, and newer stars such as Madonna and U2. Each act would be given 20 minutes to perform—for no money. Nevertheless, Queen rented London's Shaw Theater for three days of rehearsal—exactly what they would

CONTINUED ON PAGE 80

ANDRE CSILLAG, COURTESY MARK HAYWARD

LIVE AID WAS QUEEN'S rebirth, leading to three more albums and dozens more shows. The day was, and is, reason to celebrate, though now touched by sadness. Mercury was never able to reach such heights again.

MERCURY CAPTIVATED everyone that day; even his own bandmates couldn't take their eyes off him. After Queen belted out its hits—"We Are the Champions," and "We Will Rock You" among them—Mercury's father, Bomi Bulsara, watching from home, turned to his wife and Mercury's mom, Jer, and said, "Our boy's done it."

NEAL PRESTON

CONTINUED FROM PAGE 76

have done before a new tour. "It was a challenge because that was the first time we'd done a gig without our own lights and sound gear," May said. "We were naked. It was a test." Worse, Mercury was under doctor's orders not to sing because of recurrent throat problems. He ignored them, of course.

On July 13, 1985, Live Aid unfolded before a crowd of 70,000 (including Prince Charles and Princess Diana) in London, with 100,000 more in Philadelphia, and a billion television viewers worldwide. The Beach Boys, Elvis Costello, Led Zeppelin, and Bryan Adams (among others) had already performed—with mostly lackluster results, but just as the U.S. TV feed switched to London, Geldof heard what he called "this sound. I thought, God, who's got this sound together?" he said. "I went outside and saw that it was Queen."

The band's set began with Mercury at the piano singing "Bohemian Rhapsody." The crowd immediately began singing along, but Mercury wasn't fully aware of the connection he was making until he began the following number, "Radio Ga Ga." Looking out at the audience for the first time, he

PERHAPS THE SINGLE MOST star-studded event of the '80s, Live Aid hosted such performers as George Michael (in yellow shirt, at left), Bono and Paul McCartney (sharing a microphone), along with Mercury (middle, in red), David Bowie's backup singer Helena Springs, and Bowie. All told, Live Aid raised $125 million to fight poverty in Ethiopia.

GEORGES DE KEERLE/GAMMA-RAPHO/GETTY

saw thousands of people waving their hands, aping the song's music video. "He was dazzled by that, having never seen anything quite like it before," Peter Freestone recalled. "They had only ever performed that song in darkness."

Mercury then launched into an incendiary version of "Hammer to Fall," followed by "Crazy Little Thing Called Love" and finally (of course) "We Will Rock You" and "We Are the Champions." By this time, the crowd had become a sea of moving, singing, roaring fans. "Queen tore up the rule book and then rewrote it in 20 seconds flat," said Pete Smith, Live Aid's event coordinator. "The effect was palpable." Indeed, Elton John shouted backstage that the band had stolen the show. Watching in Feltham, Middlesex, Bomi Bulsara turned to his wife, Jer, and said, "Our boy's done it."

"They were absolutely the best band on that day," Geldof said. (They were also the loudest, their engineer having cranked the volume just before they took the stage.) In the wake of this triumph, Queen's album sales soared—along with the band's spirits. "Live Aid turned our world upside down," Deacon said. Instead of breaking up, they embarked on a new album after director Russell Mulcahy asked them to write music for his 1986 movie *Highlander.* Four of the resulting songs appeared on Queen's *A Kind of Magic,* which the band recorded in London and Munich from September 1985 to April 1986.

Released in June 1986, the album had a mixed reception. The first single, "One Vision," was criticized for supposedly hopping on the Live Aid bandwagon, and Queen itself was still on the United Nation's blacklist for playing apartheid South Africa in 1984.

QUEEN WAS KING AGAIN IN 1986, with Mercury up to his old tricks onstage (here, at Wembley Stadium) even as rumors circulated about his deteriorating health.

DENIS O'REGAN/PREMIUM/GETTY

Nevertheless, the band began a sold-out 26-date European tour that summer. On July 12, their concert at Wembley Stadium was recorded for a live double album, *Queen at Wembley.* On August 9, they played a two-hour set before 120,000 fans at Knebworth Park. It was their biggest audience ever—and, sadly, their last. Within a year, Mercury would be too weak to tour.

On October 12, Mercury and Jim Hutton were returning to London from a Japanese vacation when they saw a tabloid headline: QUEEN STAR FREDDIE IN AIDS SHOCK. Though the story claimed that Mercury *wasn't* infected by the virus, the singer snapped when pressed about the issue by a reporter: "Do I look like I'm dying of AIDS? Now leave me alone."

Still, Mercury had reason to be concerned. Though he'd previously claimed he'd been tested and found HIV-negative, his story changed in April 1987, when he called Hutton—then visiting his parents in Ireland—and revealed that he had AIDS. "The doctors have taken a big lump out of me," he said of the biopsy that had revealed the illness. (Hutton was also later diagnosed with HIV. He died of lung cancer in 2010.)

Mercury could have been HIV positive for almost a decade, given the virus's long gestation period. "He claimed he was diagnosed with HIV/AIDS in 1987," Mark Langthorne said, "but when you later learn that in fact he was likely infected five years earlier, you see a different person than the one you thought you saw. You see a person fighting."

Though Mercury continued to deny his illness, he couldn't hide the symptoms. While recording a collaboration with his favorite singer, the opera diva Montserrat Caballé, he showed up covered in Kaposi's sarcoma lesions, purplish bruise-like blotches common in AIDS patients. "It's all right, dear!" he told one alarmed observer. "There's no need to look at me like that. I've just been drinking too much vodka and doing too much. The doctors say I have a liver complaint."

Of course, his fellow bandmates knew the truth, though none mentioned it—until Mercury did. During the recording of their 13th studio album, *The Miracle,* he broke the news to the band, Taylor told *Rolling Stone.* "You probably realize what my problem is," Mercury said. "Well, that's it and I don't want it to make a difference. I don't want it to be known. I don't want to talk about it. I just want to get on and work until I f---ing well drop. I'd like you to support me in this."

As a result of Mercury's confession, the recording sessions for *The Miracle* were unprecedentedly civil, though May suffered an emotional breakdown. "My dad died at the same time and my marriage broke up, so for a while I felt that I didn't exist as a person," he said. "I'd look in the mirror and think 'Oh, he looks all right, he's a rock star.' But inside there was almost nothing there." May was so depressed that, some days, he couldn't even get out of his chair in the studio. "I don't know how I got through it," he said.

When they were finished recording, Freddie returned to Garden Lodge, his London home—and to the staff and entourage that he called "the Real Life"—for the last time. With paparazzi surrounding the house, he tried to lose himself in the art he had abandoned after college. "He would sit for hours trying to do a portrait of Delilah," Freestone later said of the beloved cat that had inspired Mercury's song of the same name. "It proved too much for him. But he did manage a couple of abstracts. That was down to Matisse. We were looking through an auction catalogue one day, and there was a Matisse going for £10,000. 'Ten grand?' cried Freddie. '*I* could do that!'"

Though Mercury refused most visitors, his bandmates, his parents, Elton John, and Mary Austin came to see him. A particularly uplifting encounter came courtesy of comedian Mike Myers, who was then filming *Wayne's World,* a movie based on a popular *Saturday Night Live* sketch about a metal-music fan who hosts a cable TV show. The

DENIS O'REGAN/PREMIUM/GETTY

THOUGH HIS BANDMATES KNEW, no one spoke of it—until Mercury did. While recording their 13th album, *The Miracle,* he officially delivered the news to the three other men: He was sick with AIDS. Though it wasn't yet acknowledged, he was likely already ill here in Europe on the Magic Tour, in the summer of '86.

DENIS O'REGAN/PREMIUM/GETTY

film opens with Wayne (Myers) and his friends lip-synching and head-banging to "Bohemian Rhapsody." Though the film wasn't finished, Myers showed a clip of the scene to May, who brought it to Mercury. "Freddie loved it," the guitarist said. "He just laughed and thought it was great, this little video. The funny thing was, we always regarded the song as tongue-in-cheek ourselves."

On May 22, 1989, *The Miracle* was released on the heels of its first single, "I Want It All," which became a UK No. 1. Though May had written the song, the band had agreed to share all songwriting credits for the first time. "I think Freddie and I squashed Roger and John in the beginning," May confessed. "We were the major songwriters, and we didn't give them enough say. Now it's totally equal."

Nevertheless, the album's songs were nothing if not personal—including "Scandal," which reflected the band's battles with the tabloids, and "Was It All Worth It," which asked: "What is there left for me to do in this life? / Did I achieve what I had set in my sights? / Am I a happy man or is this sinking sand? / Was it all worth it?" In the end, Mercury's answer is yes.

Immediately after *The Miracle* was released, Mercury told the band he wanted to start making another album. "Freddie felt that was the best way to keep his spirits up," Taylor said. "We backed him right up to the hilt. *Innuendo* was made very much on borrowed time." (During the recording, a white American rapper named Vanilla Ice shamelessly sampled the bass line from "Under Pressure" on "Ice Ice Baby" without attributing—or paying—Bowie or Queen. The case was settled out of court, with Bowie and Queen receiving an undisclosed sum and songwriting credits in perpetuity.)

Respecting Mercury's wishes, the band didn't talk about his illness. "We hid everything," May said. "I guess we lied! Because we were trying to protect him." The issue remained unspoken even among themselves, though May's "The Show Must Go On" and Taylor's "These Are the Days of Our Lives" were "things that we gave to Freddie as a way of him working through stuff with us," May said. "And that wasn't spoken. It was us trying to find the end before we got there."

SUZIE GIBBONS/REDFERNS/GETTY

FEW COULD MAKE AN ENTRANCE like Queen—in 1986, as part of the Magic Tour, the band surprised fans at Knebworth Park in Hertfordshire by arriving via helicopter. Later, Mercury and Taylor gave them their money's worth, here. No one—certainly not Mercury—could have known that that night in August would be his last-ever performance.

MERCURY'S FUNERAL ON November 29, 1991, was short (25 minutes), small, and private. The surviving bandmates of Queen remembered him as the "most beloved member of our family." His home in London was a message board for fans for years; in 2017, Mary Austin, who still lives there, wiped away all messages, saying she was sick of her home being "defaced."

BRIDGEMAN IMAGES

Recording *Innuendo* was a surprisingly uplifting experience, according to May. "Freddie was in pain, but inside the studio there was a sort of blanket around, and he could be happy and enjoy what he liked doing best," he said. "Sometimes it would only last a couple of hours a day because he would get very tired. But during that couple of hours, boy, would he give a lot. When he couldn't stand up, he used to prop himself up against a desk and down a vodka: 'I'll sing it till I f---king bleed.'"

Released in January 1991, the title track off *Innuendo* reached No. 1 in the UK—the band's first chart-topper in a decade. In February, the album reached No. 1 in the UK and became the band's first U.S. gold record since *The Works*. But the archival Queen performances that were used in the video for "The Show Must Go On" further fueled rumors of Mercury's illness. The band continued to deny the problem, even though Mercury could hardly walk during the recording of the song. Still, "he went in and killed it, completely lacerated that vocal," May later said.

The last song Mercury ever recorded was "Mother Love," a plaintive plea for "comfort and care" made in May 1991. During the sessions, the singer could hardly stand. "I don't know where he found the energy," May said. "Probably from vodka. He would get in the mood, do a little warm up then say, 'Give me my shot.' He'd swig it down ice cold. Stolichnaya, usually. Then he would say, 'Roll the tape.' He still had astonishing power in his lungs at that point, I really don't know where it came from. The song starts low and gentle, but Mercury chose to push himself and go higher. We looked at each other and knew there was a mountain to climb. That's when the vodka really went down. He said, 'I will hit these notes.' And he did. It was a wonderful performance."

Mercury had recorded everything but the song's last verse when he stopped because he wasn't feeling well. "I think I should call it a day now," he said. "I will finish it when I come back, next time."

He never made it.

On November 23, 1991, Mercury released a statement confirming that he had AIDS. Less than 24 hours later, he died of bronchial pneumonia, a complication of AIDS. Dave Clark, a longtime friend and leader of the '60s group the Dave Clark Five, gave this version of Mercury's last moments: "He just

STEWART MARK/CAMERA PRESS/REDUX

MEXICO
TORREON
GARDEN LODGE
I STILL LOVE YOU
13.7.93
WE TOO, HANNES!
ALSO ROMAN
+KARLI
GREG
MARCO
FREDDIE
MY HEART
LOVE OF MY LIFE
MISS YOU FREDDIE
FREDDIE
IVA a JITKA
4.6.93
MITO
JOHN '93
IN OUR HEARTS

sat up, I held him and he smiled and he had gone. He had been so brave. Only a handful of people knew just how ill Freddie had become. But Freddie wanted it that way."

Freestone then called Taylor, who was on his way to see Mercury. "Don't bother coming," he said.

On November 27, Mercury's funeral was held at West London's Kensal Green. In keeping with his family's faith, it was a Zoroastrian service, though Mercury had long ago left the religion behind. Flowers filled five Daimler hearses, while Mercury's body was transported in a Rolls Royce. Aretha Franklin sang "You've Got a Friend," and Montserrat Caballé performed Freddie's favorite piece of music: "D'Amor sull'ali rosee" from Verdi's *Il Trovatore*.

Several people were conspicuously absent: Jim Hutton and Austrian actress Barbara Valentin had been barred from the service—likely by Austin, to whom Mercury had left Garden Lodge, along with the bulk of his estate. To this day, she lives in the mansion, where Mercury's decor remains unchanged. "Even in death I care about him and hope he's okay," she said. "I felt married to Freddie. I loved him very much."

Still, Mercury's most significant affair was with his public. Not long after his death, "Bohemian Rhapsody" was rereleased, along with "These Are the Days of Our Lives" as a double A-side single. At the end of the music video for "Days," the star looks straight into the camera and says, "I still love you." It was his final moment on film.

"He quit while he was ahead," said Valentin, who died of a stroke in 2002. "He used to tell me that you can never afford to fall from the top, be not as great as you once were. Fame had made

IT WAS NEVER THE SAME without Mercury, but the show goes on. In 2018, May played the 02 Arena in London with *American Idol* heartthrob Adam Lambert (here). In 2005, May and Paul Rodgers (right) played Olympia Hall in Munich; in December of that year, May and his wife, actress Anita Dobson, and two kids (Louisa and Jimmy) were the picture of pride after Queen Elizabeth named him a Commander of the Order of the British Empire at Buckingham Palace (bottom).

MATTHEW BAKER/GETTY

JOERG KOCH/AFP/GETTY

FIONA HANSON/PA/GETTY

him the loneliest person in the world. To compensate for this, his life became wilder and wilder, until it controlled him. He was overcompensating for his loneliness: Freddie did everything to extremes. The price he paid was the most terrible. I know he wouldn't have planned a life like that. But he got his way. Immortality was what he wanted, and immortality was what he got."

ONE YEAR AFTER MERCURY'S death, the first clinical trials of combination therapies to treat HIV infection were conducted, and the FDA licensed the first rapid HIV test—advances that would eventually make the disease manageable instead of a death sentence. It's tempting to think that, if Mercury had lived a little longer, he might have survived. "He missed it by just a few months," May said. "If it had been a bit later, he would still have been with us, I'm sure."

Queen effectively disbanded after Mercury's death, its three remaining members trying to redefine their lives apart from the band. (May returned to astronomy, writing books and eventually completing the Ph.D. thesis he'd given up on after Queen took off.) But they reunited for Mercury's sake on April 20, 1992. "We made the announcement that we were going to do a tribute concert... to send him out in the style which he deserved," May said. A benefit for the Mercury Phoenix Trust, a charity that Austin had established to raise money for AIDS organizations, the Freddie Mercury Tribute Concert was performed in front of 72,000 people at Wembley Stadium. George Michael, Roger Daltrey, Def Leppard, and many others performed—along with the three surviving Queen members.

IN 2002, TAYLOR AND MAY (left) accepted a star on Hollywood Boulevard (it reads "Queen," of course). In the 2018 movie *Bohemian Rhapsody,* Rami Malek stars as Mercury.

L. COHEN/WIREIMAGE/GETTY

NICK DELANEY/© 20TH CENTURY FOX/COURTESY EVERETT

David Bowie surprised the crowd by reciting the Lord's Prayer on his knees, and Guns N' Roses front man Axl Rose dueted with Elton John on "Bohemian Rhapsody," which had recently become a hit all over again—thanks to the success of *Wayne's World.*

In 1995, Queen released *Made in Heaven,* which featured Mercury's final recordings—including "Mother Love." It became the band's ninth No. 1 in the UK and sold 20 million copies worldwide. On its cover, Freddie is shown pumping his right fist into the air over Lake Geneva—a stance reflected in the statue of the singer that was unveiled in Montreux in November 1996, almost five years to the day after his death. The tribute on the statue's plaque was written by May: "Lover of Life, Singer of Songs."

In 1997, May, Taylor, and Deacon performed "The Show Must Go On" with Elton John at the Paris premiere of Maurice Béjart's *Ballet for Life,* which featured several Queen songs and was dedicated in part to Mercury. It would be Deacon's final live performance with Queen: He retired immediately afterward—despite Elton John's insistence that, well, the show must go on. "You guys should go out and play again," he told Queen. "It must be like having a Ferrari in the garage waiting for a driver."

No one could ever replace Mercury, of course—no one even tried—but in 2004 Queen teamed up with Paul Rodgers, the British singer best known for his work with Bad Company. Calling themselves Queen + Paul Rodgers, they toured on and off until amicably parting in 2009. Taylor later admitted that the singer may have wearied of the band's perfectionism. "Brian

and I go to incredible lengths to get things right," he said. "He'd never met two pickier, fussier individuals." Some things never change.

The same year Rodgers left the lineup, a young singer named Adam Lambert auditioned for TV's *American Idol* by singing "Bohemian Rhapsody." In the show's season's finale, Lambert (who finished as the runner-up) performed "We Are the Champions" with May and Taylor, which led to them touring as Queen + Adam Lambert. "I always wonder if Freddie is looking down on us, excited that the times have changed," Lambert said. "I hope I'm carrying on his legacy in a way that would make him proud and that he would get a kick out of. And I hope he's envious of my footwear collection."

But Mercury himself wasn't entirely finished. In 2014, Queen released *Queen Forever,* which featured three new songs with Mercury vocals—along with "There Must Be More to Life than This," a duet between Mercury and Michael Jackson. The album felt disposable—Taylor called it "bloody miserable"—but was a modest hit.

In recent years, the Queen legacy has expanded to include a hit jukebox musical (*We Will Rock You*), an official tribute band (The Queen Extravaganza), and now a movie. Starring Rami Malek as Mercury, *Bohemian Rhapsody* tells the story of the band's formation up to its 1985 Live Aid performance. "Here's a man that would sing 'We Are the Champions' in an arena to thousands of people and they're all singing it back to him," Malek said. "His ability to unify people, no matter who they are, was so far ahead of its time. I can't think of anyone else who was capable of that." ●

PHIL DENT/REDFERNS/GETTY

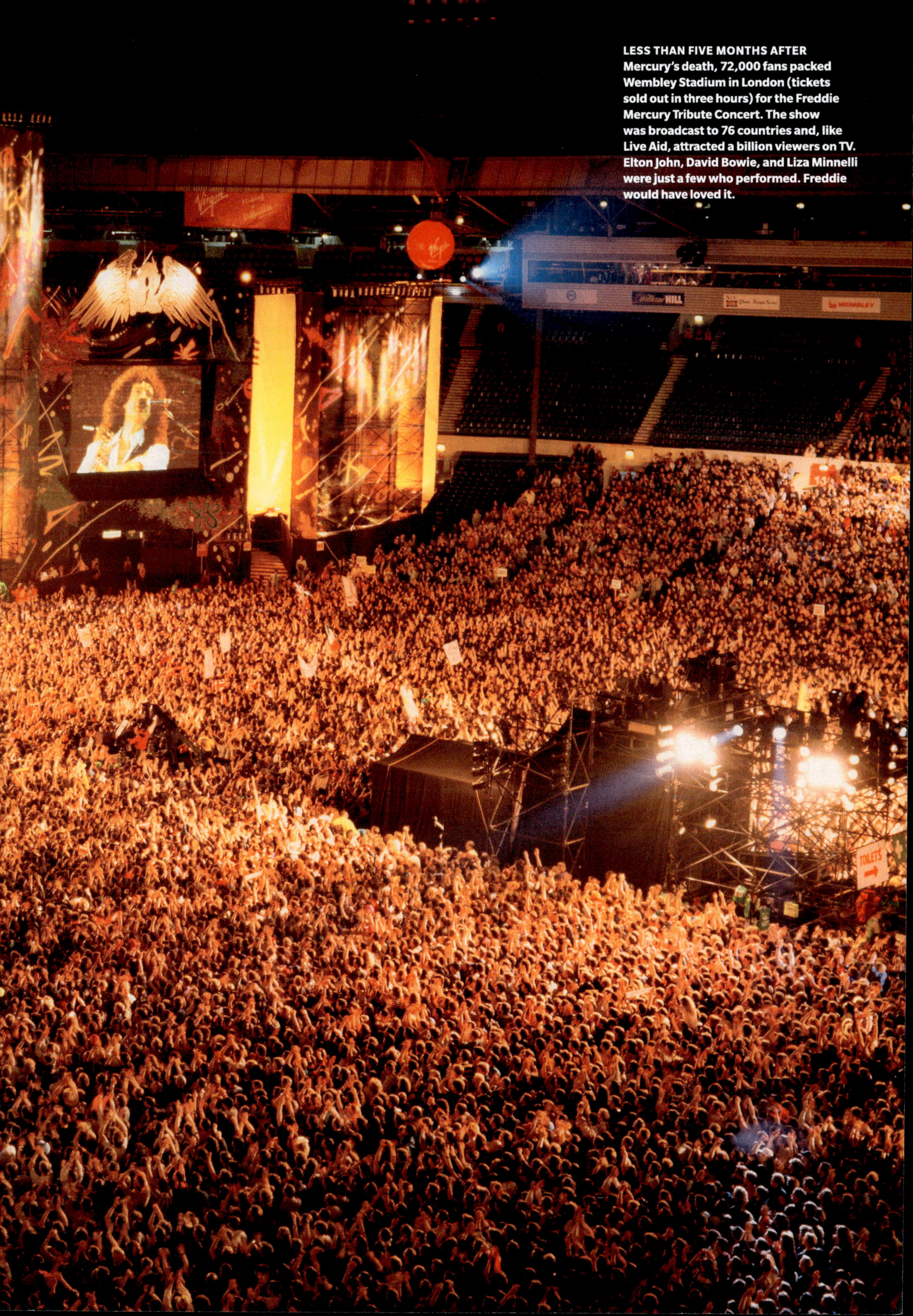

LESS THAN FIVE MONTHS AFTER Mercury's death, 72,000 fans packed Wembley Stadium in London (tickets sold out in three hours) for the Freddie Mercury Tribute Concert. The show was broadcast to 76 countries and, like Live Aid, attracted a billion viewers on TV. Elton John, David Bowie, and Liza Minnelli were just a few who performed. Freddie would have loved it.

"Freddie is great. At a time when everybody around was doing God knows what, Queen was making music."
—OZZY OSBOURNE
NEAL PRESTON

Made in the USA
Columbia, SC
31 July 2019